Returning
to *Radiance*

Returning
to *Radiance*

Tapping into the dancing light
of your inner grace, beauty, and compassion

Fr. Francis Chun, S.T.L.

Paschal Peace Press

RETURNING TO RADIANCE
Copyright © 2018 by Francis H. Chun

Paschal Peace Press

Cover and book designed by Tony Tarr

ISBN: 978-0-692-97902-0
Library of Congress Control Number: 2017919243

1. Self-help   2. Relationships   3. Spirituality   4. Prayer

With profound gratitude this book
is dedicated to The Holy Spirit, Who is the
Source of true wisdom and radiance.

*A special thanks to Tony Tarr, for the
typesetting, for designing both covers,
for designing the entire book!*

A big thanks to Leanne Mills (YourLadyinRED)
and Br. Thomas Di Novo for all their help.

Endorsments

"Returning to Radiance" can change a person's life.

As a dedicated student of Father Chun, it was with gratitude and acceptance of God's love and mercy first to myself by using the tools of this book. Now in one place I had all the lessons I had scribbled on pages and pages of notes taken during his retreats and homilies. But now it made sense as each lesson was tied into Sacred Scripture and allowed me to zero in to the areas of my own brokenness that had built up residue over time. Fr Chun's book "Returning to Radiance" was like "Holy Windex" that in 6 short months cleaned the inner walls of my soul. Certainly confession over the years would absolve me of my "sins" in the way I reacted and mishandled situations in relationships. However, I didn't have the practical help and discernment ability from God because of what I call spiritual residue. All the self-help books on relationships never helped me.

With my new improved attitude of love and forgiveness of myself first, I have been able to see through God's eyes and show and share with others the compassion and inner peace I have found; starting with my own family, and then allowing God to use me in humility, simplicity and charity to serve others. *(From the Foreword).*

As I started to read through the book I realized the important fact, I was not alone. The Holy Spirit was there all along, and somewhere inside my self-pity and hurt, I heard the words Father Chun so carefully crafted. It was like he had written the words especially for me. As I read each chapter, I became more and more aware, that it was not my wife or anyone else that was holding me back, or creating the messed up life I found myself in - it was me! I was in control of my own radiance, and all I needed was a path to understand and find it. His prayers, quizzes, examples and breathing exercises in this book were like landmarks along the path that I needed to take, to return to my radiance, and eventually to the radiance that my wife and I once had in our marriage.

My relationships with others now have never been stronger. It's amazing when you have the Holy Spirit inside all your intentions, how it affects the people in your life in the most positive way. The experience is unlike any other.
(From the Preface)

Forward

It is beautiful how the Holy Spirit works... as just last night I knew which testimony (as there have been so many blessings) I was meant to share.

I had been inspired to help my son with transportation to different locations the past several weeks, willingly working my daily schedule to accommodate his equipment to job sites. This was just one of many kindnesses we had been moved recently to extend this 22yr old son of mine. We had opened up our home again last spring to not only him, but his dog as well (my husband hates pets) to give him a place to stay and recover from knee surgery, because he couldn't work, and afford food and rent elsewhere.

So last night after picking him up and bringing him home, we are met at the door by my husband lovingly bringing his dog out for a potty and to greet us (a common sight these days, because he had read this book too)!

But the fruits from me embracing this book "Returning to Radiance" written by the "Q&A" Priest, Fr. Chun, could not have been more radically exemplified but through the words out of this son's mouth just last night as I was in the kitchen with him.

He and my husband had just been discussing the broken shower head and instantly, though tired from working all day, my son jumped up, grabbed his tools and fixed it. Then returning to the kitchen (out of the blue) he says with such love in his eyes, "Oh Mom, you will never have to worry about someone always taking care of you, for no one could take better care of you than me!" Then he gave me a tender hug and kiss on the cheek. I knew he was speaking from his heart. This declaration of love came after the past couple of days of him coming in my room, flopping on my bed and allowing me to hold and cuddle him for about 5-10 min as he shared about the work he had done the prior day. But displays of love and affection hadn't happened for years between us, not since back when he was really little.

Yes, I'm speaking about the same troubled, angry, bitter and hateful one that had rained terror out of his pain, upon our family for the past number of years. Outbursts of rage towards each of us. Breaking glass tables and almost putting his younger brother through the glass back door during one nasty altercation. Neighbors and friends alike had witnessed his self-destruction and verbal abuse of us in horror and pity. This same child that had tattooed my initials on his forearm years before (though it seemed odd when his actions towards me were contrary). Yes, I had done the same tattoo of his initials on my right wrist (that I would always kiss after my blessing at Mass). But mine were to remind me to not hate or fear him, but to pray like St Monica and keep loving him, in pure faith and trust. This was especially hard these past 7 years when his life was being lived in darkness. In and out of jail and frequent visits from the police to quell one of his incidents used to be the norm. Yes, the same one that we even had to take legal action and have evicted from our home less than 2 years ago!

So what changed?

I did!

As a dedicated student of Father Chun, it was with gratitude and acceptance of "God's love and mercy" first to myself by using the tools of this book.

Now in one place I had all the lessons I had scribbled on pages and pages of notes taken during his retreats and homilies. But now it made sense, as each lesson was tied into Sacred Scripture, and allowed me to zero in to the areas of my own brokenness that had built up residue over time. Father Chun's book "Returning to Radiance" was like "Holy Windex" that in 6 short months cleaned the inner walls of my soul. Certainly confession over the years would absolve me of my "sins" in the way I reacted and mishandled situations in relationships. However, I didn't have the practical help and discernment ability from God because of what I call spiritual residue. All the self-help books on relationships never helped me. Sure I prayed but God's total healing power wasn't able to flow through me and bring about the spiritual transformation needed. I knew the abundance God wanted for me, but I would limit it with my own negative self-talk, and inability to understand the pain I would cause those around me with my insecurities. Always praying for God to fix "them" or take away some problem I was facing. But suffering and challenges are a part of life. Everyone has them, though they may be different in appearance.

With my new improved attitude of love and forgiveness of myself first, I have been able to see through God's eyes and show and share with others the compassion and inner peace I have found starting with my own family, and then allowing God to use me in humility, simplicity and charity to serve others. May we all be open vessels to bring God's Mercy to the world. And as the song says, "let it begin with me"!

Leanne Mills - YourLadyinRED

Preface

It was hard facing the real world in my relationship with my wife, as our marriage headed for the rocks. I found I was retreating back into myself, when situations got too overwhelming, rather than trying to deal with them directly. I felt like I was alone in my struggle, always looking for self-pity, rather than facing the problems straight on. We were not even communicating with focus or honesty and I was at a loss and knew our relationship was suffering terribly. Around the time it had hit rock bottom, Father Chun asked me to help him on this book. My first reaction was "why me - I have no idea right now what the word *Radiance* even means, let alone return to it." All I could think about was myself and all the problems we were having as a couple. I was definitely not in the right state of mind to take on a project like this.

In steps the Holy Spirit. Father Chun said, "think about it", and left the first draft with me to review, to see if I would be interested in working on the project. I actually thought little about it. I put the copy in my back pack, and headed down to LA, to be with my sister, to get a fresh look at my life.

As I started to read through the book, I realized the important fact, I was not alone. The Holy Spirit was there all along, and somewhere inside my self-pity and hurt, I heard the words Father Chun so carefully crafted. It was like he had written the words especially for me. As I read each chapter, I became more and more aware, that it was not my wife or anyone else that was holding me back, or creating the messed up life I found myself in. It was me. I was in control of my own radiance, and all I needed was a path to understand and find it. His prayers, quizzes, examples and breathing exercises were like landmarks along the path that I needed to take, to return to my radiance, and eventually to the radiance that my wife and I once had in our marriage.

And it didn't just stop there; all my relationships changed because of this book. I no longer waited for the world to make its first step - I was convinced to create the steps myself. Each step I took I felt like the Holy Spirit lifted me along three more steps. I sat for the next four days reading, re-reading and practicing what Father Chun so carefully created.

It's been almost eight months since we started this project, and my life has completely changed because of it. I cut back on all the worrying and responsibility I thought I needed to have in social media and worldly issues and started focusing on the spirit inside - the one that had been there all along.

My relationships with others now have never been stronger. It's amazing when you have the Holy Spirit inside all your intentions, how it affects the people in your life in the most positive way. The experience is unlike any other.

I remember how I felt from an example he uses in the book of Mother Teresa. She was able to accomplish the things in her life by allowing the Holy Spirit to guide her through simple little tasks done well every day. I am amazed how this book set off a series of re-alignments for me. It has helped to create a meaning for me that will remain with me for the rest of my life.

Thank you for this opportunity, Father Chun.

Tony Tarr

Table of contents

Part II
Radiance in Turmoil

Part III
Radiance of Loving

Part IV
Radiance Through Prayer

Introduction

This is a manual, a workbook, for re-reading and to be experienced. Use it as a handy reference for living a life enhanced with inner peace and creativity. The Mother of Learning is Repetition.

The content of this workbook flows from the practical wisdom of Zen Buddhism, Psychology, Philosophy, and Christian Spirituality. The most effective form of psycho-therapy is cognitive-behavioral therapy – a combination of cognitive therapy and behavioral modification. This manual will help you to change some of your attitudes and help you to make beneficial behavioral changes.

The effectiveness of this workbook will be measured by how you share with others what you learn from it. In living life, it is not how fast you run or how high you climb, but how you love and help others. Use this manual well and your beneficial influence on others will brighten their lives.

Part I

Radiance in Darkness

What determines my fate — misery or inner peace — is not the tragedy of the past and the difficult circumstances of the present, but my attitude towards both, and how I deal with past pain and present situations.

Prelude: Healing and Peace

The human heart can ache for many reasons:

Missing someone deceased who was always there for you, such as a parent, child, spouse, or friend. The death of a beloved is also the death of the hopes and expectations associated with that person.

Missing certain shared activities — social, marital, sexual — with a person who is no longer with you because of divorce. Missing the love, support, and comfort you craved that should have been there for you as a child but were not.

Although human living always involves loss and suffering, each person is unique with unique situations, so each heart aches differently.

A heart wounded by abandonment or betrayal that is unexpected, unimagined will continue to fester until healing takes place. Since every person and relationship is unique, every healing will occur differently.

Recovering from trauma is heroic. A person who lives a "normal" life despite trauma is more of a hero than a war hero, who is a hero for a few hours or a day. A person suffering from trauma who carries on is a hero for decades.

But recovering from trauma is only the first step to healing, wholeness, holiness. (Every saint had a dark past; every sinner can have a bright future.)

When the heart wounded by trauma aches, the entire person needs healing. But being healed does not mean you will no longer feel sad or hurt. (As you will see later, all negative emotions are good.) Being healed means that the positive emotions of living will predominate over the negative emotions, which will be accepted as good and beneficial anyway. After being healed, a person must shift from the survival mode of existing to living fully.

Being healed enables a person to live and enjoy life more fully.

You will learn to accept whatever feelings/thoughts that come without analyzing or resisting them, whether they be pleasant or unpleasant. You will learn to transform the loss and suffering of living into benefits for yourself and for others.

Overview

$\mathcal{A}$. Lost in a Dark Jungle

a. A dark jungle of pain

No one deliberately sets out to become lost in a dangerous jungle. Yet some people end up being lost in a dark jungle of pain that is full of fears, anxieties, and continual tension. When a person is lost in such a dark jungle of pain, how can he find his way out to a life open to the light of peace, healing, and delight?

Physical and emotional pain can be a vicious cycle: when it hurts, I tense up. When I tense up, it hurts more and longer. Then the vicious cycle continues on and on.

I have to break out of this vicious cycle of pain. Resistance begets resistance. Because what I resist will persist, I will neither deny my pain nor fight it. I will accept the pain and learn to live with it. By doing this, pain will have less power over me. My attention magnifies whatever I focus on. Focusing on my depression makes it more important than it really is, and makes me more depressed and lasts longer.

Focusing on my aching heart makes it ache more and longer. I will live my life as best as I can, and focus on the present tasks at hand.

By doing this, the ache will be pushed to the edge of my awareness, and often disappear from my awareness. A prolonged sense of being a helpless victim makes my heart ache all the more.

I will take control over my inner life because I have the power to focus my attention on whatever I want, and to choose my external activities. There is only one person who can relieve the continuous aching of my-heart, and eventually heal it — myself!

I can and I will leave this jungle of pain.

b. Darkness from the past

When I drag the pain of the past into my present pain and project both into the thought of future pain, I weave a wider web of pain that enmeshes my entire life.

Memories of past pain joined to my present fears and hopeless expectations have the power to crush my spirit if I allow this to happen.

I will not allow this to happen! I will learn how to drop the past by refusing to focus on it. I will pay no attention to thoughts about the non-existing future.

What determines my fate — misery or inner peace -- is not the tragedy of the past and the difficult circumstances of the present, but my attitude towards both, and how I deal with past pain and present situations.

Because the past events that caused the pain no longer exist, I will not bring them back to life by recalling them or thinking about them.

If painful events come to mind, I will dismiss them by focusing on something else.

Because worrying about the future won't change it, I will stop doing this useless, depressing practice.

Because people who have a why will find a how, I will keep renewing my commitment to my family and friends.

c. Lost in darkness - (t/f Quiz 1)

1 ◯ The past does not exist.

2 ◯ The events of my past do not exist.

3 ◯ Some people allow the stress of the past to aggravate the stress of the present.

4 ◯ A major part of me is the accumulative result of all my past experiences.

5 ◯ The future does not exist in reality.

6 ◯ Anxieties about the future can increase the stress of the present.

Answers

1. True. The past does not exist. **True**. The past does not exist. It is over with in reality, but may exist in one's memory.

2. True. The events of my past do not exist. **True**. These events do not exist in reality, but their residual effects do exist in us.

3. True. Some people allow the stress of the past to aggravate the stress of the present. **True**. Anxieties about how my past affects me aggravate the stress of the present in my relationships and and my work.

4. True. A major part of me is the accumulative result of all my past experiences. **True**. I am the result of my past.

5. True. The future does not exist in reality. **True**. It may exist only in my mind or in my imagination. It will become real only when it becomes the present.

6. True. Anxieties about the future can increase the stress of the present. **True**. Anxieties about coming events can double the stress a person is experiencing.

c. *Lost in darkness* (continued) - *t/f Quiz*

7 ◯   Past events and future events are beyond my control.

8 ◯   Only some aspects of my present situation are within my control.

9 ◯   What can enhance and imporve my life exists only in the present.

10 ◯   Denying past events results in turmoil.

7. **True**. Past events and future events are beyond my control. **True**. How can I reach back to the non-existing events of my past? How can I reach out to the non-existing events of the future?

8. **True**. Only some aspects of my present situation are within my control. **True**. The great majority of things are beyond my control; i.e., the laws of Physics and Biology, what other people think, say or do. However, I can control what I think, say, decide, and do.

9. **True**. What can enhance and improve my life exists only in the present. **True**. *Real* benefits exist only in the present.

10. **True**. Denying past events results in turmoil. **True**. Denying what happened goes against reality. True peace rests on reality.

d. The hazards of darkness

Whenever I revisit the hurts and wounds of the past, I am wandering in the circles of the past that lead to a dead end.

Whenever I worry about the future or dread the future, I am following the false trail of a future that doesn't exist.

I will take the path of the present. I will focus my attention on the present task at hand.

Whenever I focus on injustices suffered, mistreatment from others, or past trauma, I entangle myself in the vines of self-pity.

I will focus on the positive aspects of my life. I will talk about the positive aspects of my life.

Whenever I blame myself for the past, or cling to my feelings of guilt, I risk slipping into the swamp of guilt feelings. I will let go of my guilt feelings by refusing to give them my attention. I will drop feelings of guilt by refusing to recall my failings, by refusing to focus on my mistakes.

Whenever I try to control the things that are beyond my control, and neglect to use the control I do have over myself, I keep falling into the pits of frustrations. I will learn to accept or ignore things beyond my control.

e. The hazards of the past

The past events of my life no longer exist. They're gone.

I bear the residual effects of my past, but I will not allow the stress of my past to seep into my present situations.

After complete acceptance of past pain and suffering, there is no need for me to focus on the pain of the past.

Focusing on the distress or pain of the past only contaminates my present situations.

I will empty my mind and heart of the bad or painful events of my past through relaxation techniques or exercises.

I will ignore and deflect feelings and reactions from the past by focusing completely on the present task at hand.

I will drop and leave these dead weights of the past.
I will attend to the present

f. The radiance of the present and the future

My brain, heart, and emotional life have the built in capability to heal itself if I give them the opportunity to heal.

My brain is its own designer, engineer, chemist, and healer. My brain is continually remaking and renewing itself.

Complete relaxation allows my brain to heal and renew itself.

When really slowed down, my heart has been designed for healing the damages inflicted by past suffering.

Relaxation techniques can heal my emotional life of the damages inflicted by trauma and tragedies of the past.

Stress can worsen physical pain, increase emotional distress, magnify suffering.

Daily calming of my mind, heart, and emotions will restore them to wellness.

I must prevent and dissolve stress for inner peace and for healing.

Relaxation techniques can cause my ingrained wellness to spring up and flow into my mind, heart, and emotions for healing and for peace within.

The past does not exist. The past does not exist. It is over with.

$\mathcal{B}$. The Darkness Within

a. The turmoil of darkness - (t/f Quiz 2)

1 ◯ All stress is good.

2 ◯ Medically, heart attacks are the number one killer in the USA.

3 ◯ We can be physically relaxed but psychologically tense.

4 ◯ We are most relaxed when asleep.

1. True. All stress is good. **True**. Stress is part of human living; it is unavoidable. Depending on one's attitude toward stress and how one deals with it, stress can lead to harmful results or beneficial results.

2. False. Medically, heart attacks are the number one killer in the USA. **False**. Medically, the number one killer in our country is hypertension (high blood pressure) which leads to heart attacks, strokes, heart failure, kidney failure.

3. False. We can be physically relaxed but psychologically tense. **False**. When we are psychologically tense, some part of our muscles automatically tense up.

4. False. We are most relaxed when asleep. **False**. Our external senses and inner faculties are functioning during sleep. Sounds and light affect our sleep. We throw off the blanket when it gets too warm; we hear the alarm clock that wakes us up. We dream every night about every 90 minutes. During this REM (dreaming) sleep, our inner faculties of memory, imagination, emotions, and simple reasoning are active.
If some of our muscles are tense when we fall asleep, they remain partially tense throughout the **night** – this is the reason we sometimes wake up feeling more tired than when we went to bed.

a. The turmoil of darkness (continued) - t/f Quiz

5 ◯ Entertainment = relaxation.

6 ◯ We can lower our blood pressure without medication.

7 ◯ Most Americans resort to entertainment for relaxation.

8 ◯ We can control and change the way we feel.

9 ◯ We can be psychologically relaxed, but physically tense.

10 ◯ Our emotions can cause much stress in our daily living.

Answers

5. False. Entertainment = relaxation. **False**. The only form of entertainment that is truly relaxing may be listening to soothing music while in a relaxed state.

6. True. We can lower our blood pressure without medication. **True**. Lowering one's blood pressure without medication through proper diet and regular exercise is a long-term process. Doing slow deep breathing for five minutes or longer will lower one's blood pressure in the short term.

7. True. Most Americans resort to entertainment for relaxation. **True**. Americans are among the most stressed out people on earth, because they confuse entertainment with relaxation and don't know how to truly relax.

8. True. We can control and change the way we feel. **True**. The important practical question is how to do it. Refer to "Notes on Emotions". (pages 28, 29)

9. True. We can be psychologically relaxed, but physically tense. **True**. Examples of this are walking or jogging or lap swimming *with the mind free of anxious thoughts or worries.*

10. True. Our emotions can cause much stress in our daily living. **True**. Examples of this situation are common.

b. Our negative emotions - (t/f Quiz 3)

1 ◯ All negative emotions are bad.

2 ◯ We can have opposite feelings at the same time.

3 ◯ Emotions are basically non-rational, non-logical.

4 ◯ Emotions should be dealt with as separate entities in themselves.

1. False. All negative emotions are bad. **False**. We know from experience that some negative emotions are good and beneficial; e.g., fear and anger are part of our instinct for survival.

2. True. We can have opposite feelings at the same time. **True**. Two examples are: feeling fear and desire at the same time; feeling like choking and hugging a person at the same time.

3. True. Emotions are basically non-rational, non-logical. **True**. Emotions are just inner feelings that often function independently of our mind and knowledge. Our feeling part and knowing part run on *separate* but parallel tracks. But we are such rational beings that at times we try to project logical reasons into our emotions.

4. False. Emotions should be dealt with as separate entities in themselves. **False**. An entity is a separate item that stands by itself. Emotions occur in clusters like a gooey mixed-up mess. (Picture play green slime with various colors all mixed together in one gooey mess.)

b. *Our negative emotions* (continued) - *t/f Quiz*

5 ◯ Feelings of anger are natural and normal.

6 ◯ We often have feelings about feelings.

7 ◯ We should learn how to describe our emotions clearly.

8 ◯ All negative emotions are good.

5. True. Feelings of anger are natural and normal.
True. We know that feelings of anger are natural and normal. But prolonged, unresolved anger will cause problems.

6. True. We often have feelings about feelings. **True**. Some people feel guilty about feeling angry at one's spouse or one's child. Some feel guilty about feeling jealous towards a friend.

7. False. We should learn how to describe our emotions clearly. **False**. How can we describe our emotions clearly when they are non-rational, non-logical, and one gooey mess? We can state that we feel angry or feel sad, but we cannot describe clearly the feeling itself.

8. True. All negative emotions are good. **True**. Even strong anger, deep hostility, hurt feelings? Yes, *all* negative emotions are good, because all emotions are gauges that inform or warn us about what's happening. (Imagine driving a BMW without a speedometer and without a fuel gauge.)
A parallel situation: True or false, all physical pain is good. **True**. A couple living in Castle Rock, Washington has a son with the genetic defect of feeling no physical pain. The parents had to watch him as a toddler constantly, because he could put his hand in the fireplace and get a severe burn, or jump up and down even though he has a small fracture in his leg and cause a badly broken bone. Physical pain is unpleasant and undesirable, but absolutely necessary for survival, growth, and development.
Negative emotions are unpleasant and undesirable, but absolutely necessary for survival, growth, and development.

b. Our negative emotions (continued) - t/f Quiz

9 ◯ Feelings of depression are natural and normal.

10 ◯ We should deal with our negative emotions directly.

Answers

9. True. Feelings of depression are natural and normal.
True. Except for clinical depression that is long-lasting and debilitating, feelings of depression are natural and normal. Cabbages do not experience depression.

10. False. We should deal with our negative emotions directly.
False. When we try to deal with our negative emotions directly, they get stronger or last longer. When we struggle with our anger directly, the anger lasts long and may grow stronger. The best way to deal with negative emotions is to replace them with a different set of emotions. For example; the best way to remove the air from a container is to fill it with water. You cannot reach in your mind to remove undesirable thoughts or reach in your emotions to remove undesirable feelings. You can replace these undesirable thoughts and feelings with a different set of thoughts and feelings by focusing on something else and doing something else.

c. Some notes on emotions

Emotions are inner reactions to a person, situation, or event

1. Functions
    - Inform or warn you about what is happening
    - Provide opportunities for building internal strength

2. Traits
    - Non-rational, non-logical
    - No direct control
    - Temporary
    - God-given, so all are good

3. Best application of traits
    - No need to understand or describe them clearly
    - Never deal with them directly; deal with them indirectly
    - Allow time for them to settle (cool) down
    - Learn to accept all emotions (even negative ones) in
      oneself and in others

4. Comparisons:
    a. As pain is to our physical life,
       so too, negative emotions are to our psychological life.
    b. As pain is unpleasant and undesirable, but necessary
       for survival, growth, and development,
       so too negative emotions are unpleasant and
       undesirable, but necessary for survival, growth,
       and development.

5. Since all negative emotions are good,
   do not refer to emotions as "bad".
    - Emotions are positive or negative, but all are good.
    - Negative emotions are unpleasant and undesirable,
      but they are absolutely necessary for survival,
      growth, and development.

Three basic methods of dealing with emotions

1. Suppression (repression)
   - smother external expression
   - deny or not acknowledge emotion

2. Control
   - control external expression
   - acknowledge the emotion
   - use a healthy outlet (on same level)

3. Sublimation
   - control external expression
   - acknowledge the emotion
   - channel (redirect) the energy
     to a higher goal

Specific suggestions for controlling strong emotions

1. During a situation
   - control external expression
   - if possible do something else, or focus on something else
   - if possible leave situation

2. After a situation
   - allow time for emotions to calm down
   - plan ahead for the next similar situation

3. *Before a coming situation*
   - *consider the consequences of your behavior*
   - *if possible avoid the situation*
   - *control external senses and inner faculties*

Conclusion

The best way of changing the way you feel is to change your behavior to (how you respond) to others

    1. Behavior includes what you think, say and do

       2. The secret key to controlling your emotions is to control your external senses and your inner other faculties — mind, memory, imagination

$\mathcal{C}$. The Commotion of Emotions

a. Why all the commotion?

As inner reactions to a person, event, or situation, my emotions are gauges that inform or warn me about what is happening.

My emotions also provide me with opportunities for building internal strength.

By means of the flow of bio-chemicals, my emotions extend throughout all the organs of my body-mind through nerves and bundles of cells.

All my experiences of the past and memories are intertwined with the emotional network present in my body-mind.

My emotions have a life of their own,
an intelligence of their own.

The emotional flow of my life is like:
- the engine in my car
- the wind in my sail
- the colors in my favorite painting
- the rhythm in my favorite music
- the love I have for others

I will respect and accept the flow of my emotions.

b. Any bad emotions?

Like physical pain, my negative emotions are unpleasant and undesirable, but absolutely necessary for my survival, growth, and development.

Fear triggers my flight or fight response, which helps me to survive physically and psychologically.

Fear of consequences motivates me to get something done, and enables me to do it quickly to meet a deadline.

Anger helps me to set limits and to define boundaries.

Grief and sadness help me to deal with the loss of a loved one.

Hurt feelings and disappointments can help me to strengthen my relationships.

Feelings of depression can help me to develop internal strength.

I will respect and accept all my negative emotions as helpful gauges for surviving, growing, and improving my skills.

c. Flowing with the commotion

Because my emotions are non-rational, non-logical, there's no need to understand or describe them clearly.

Because I have no direct control over my emotions, I will deal with them indirectly by thinking about something else or by doing something else.

Because my emotional states are temporary, I will allow time for them to quiet and cool down.

Because all my emotions are God-given and good, I will accept all my emotions, even negative ones.

I will remind myself that there is no need for guilt feelings for having negative emotions, because all my emotions are good.

I will respect and accept all my emotions as beneficial for surviving, growing, and improving my skills.

d. Directing the inner flow

I can direct the flow of my emotions by:
- focusing my attention on this or that
- talking about this or that
- doing this or that.

*I will gain greater control over my
emotions by directing the use of my:*
- *external senses —*
  sight, hearing, smell, touch, taste

- *inner faculties —*
  *simple reasoning, memory,
  imagination, emotions*

- *spiritual powers —*
  intellect and free will

I will learn to direct the flow of my emotions to
preserve my peace within.

I will use the technique of slow breathing to
calm the commotion within.

e. Dealing with my emotions

I will use healthy outlets for my strong emotions:
- exercise or sports
- craft or hobby
- the arts
- talking it out with a friend
- positive humor

Because I have no direct control over my emotions,
I will deal with them indirectly.

Dealing with my emotions directly makes them stronger
or last longer.

*The best way of removing the air from a
container is to fill the container with water.*

I will remove my negative feelings by replacing them with
other feelings by doing something that holds my total
attention.

I will change the way I feel by changing what I'm thinking,
saying, or doing.

Life is in the breath. He who half breathes, half lives.

$\mathcal{D}$. Gathering My Resources

a. The breath of life

Arab proverb:

*"Life is in the breath.
He who half breathes, half lives."*

Shallow breathing limits my capabilities.

Deep breathing accesses my full potential.

I will use slow deep breathing:
- to gain control of my mind and body
- to be more aware
- to develop the wisdom of my body and my emotions.

My slow deep breathing will join brain, body, mind, heart, and spirit for unified effectiveness.

My slow deep breathing will strengthen the force and flow of my inner energy.

My slow deep breathing will balance the physical-emotional-mental-spiritual energy within.

b. Relaxing my body

Raise your arms straight up with palms facing frontward, and then stretch upward on tiptoes as high as you can.

Do this three times.

1. With your arms hanging as limp as wet towels, swing your arms left and right by twisting your hips and torso left and right. Do seven to ten sets of this.

2. Gently and slowly lower your head forward as far down as it will go, as if to touch your collarbone with your chin. Hold for five seconds.

3. Gently and slowly pull your head backward as far back as it will go. Hold for five seconds. Repeat this forward and backward stretching of your neck muscles three times.

4. With shoulders relaxed and arms hanging limp, rotate your head slowly in wide smooth circles seven to ten times. Then do the same thing in the opposite direction.

5. With shoulders relaxed and arms hanging limp, slowly rotate your shoulders forward in wide smooth circles seven to ten times. Do the same thing with a backward rotation.

c. A regular nightly practice

I will relax my body and calm my inner self nightly to dissolve the accumulated stress of the day:
- to fall asleep peacefully,
- to get a better night's rest,
- to wake up more refreshed.

Just before getting into bed, I will use the relaxation technique to relax my body.

After getting into bed, I will use slow deep breathing to calm my inner self.

I will do this complete relaxation technique every night as my first major step on the path to peace within.

If you usually fall asleep quickly, skip the deep breathing part.

d. Calming my inner self

After relaxing your body, sit comfortably with a straight back to balance your head, and then do deep breathing (abdominal breathing) in this manner:

I will inhale slowly from the bottom of my lungs upward for a relaxed breath, pause briefly, and then exhale slowly.

While inhaling slowly, I mentally count one;
while exhaling slowly, I mentally count one.

When I reach ten, I will begin another set of ten relaxed breaths.

Doing three, five, or more of these sets of ten breaths will: dissolve tension
- lower my blood pressure
- allow inner healing
- refresh my body, mind, heart, and spirit.

$\mathcal{E}$. A Way Out of Darkness

a. Help for the way out

To make your way out of a jungle, you need an accurate map, a guidebook, and effective tools.

The effective tools are:
- the regular nightly practice of the relaxation technique
- the daily use of the breathing technique when stressed out
- using the ABCD of stress relief before or during conflict
- dealing with emotions properly.

ABCD of stress relief
  A Accept the situation
  B Breathe deeply and slowly
  C Concentrate on the task
  D Do it well

This workbook is the Guidebook for getting out of the jungle. Use sections of it every day or whenever you need guidance.

The accurate map you need is at the end of this chapter on page 54.

If you use and apply these three aids (map, guidebook, tools) every day, you will make your way out of the jungle.

b. The radiance of the present

The stress and pressure of the present exist mainly in my mind, imagination, and emotions.

The present moment is small and manageable.

The flow of time is nature's way of preventing everything from happening all at once.

I will take a deep breath, pause, and then expel the stress and pressure of the present with my outgoing breath.

Then I will focus on my present task at hand.

Doing my present task one step at a time makes every task manageable.

In an emergency, I can do only one thing at a time. When working one step at a time, any stress experienced helps rather than hinders.

c. Obstacles to healing - (t/f Quiz 4)

1 ◯   Anger from the past can trigger anger in
present situations.

2 ◯   You cannot change another person as a person.

3 ◯   You cannot make another person happy.

4 ◯   Holding a grudge harms me more than the
other person.

5 ◯   Negative thoughts and feelings about a person mean
I still have a grudge.

1. True. Anger from the past can trigger anger in present situations. **True**. The present situation can be connected subconsciously to a similar past situation and then trigger anger in the present.

2. True. You cannot change another person as a person. **True**. A person can change only oneself *as a person*, and no one else.

3. True. You cannot make another person happy. **True**. Happiness is *a relatively stable state of living*, and not a passing emotional mood. The best one can do is to create a loving atmosphere wherein the person can be happy if he/she chooses to be happy.

4. True. Holding a grudge harms me more than the other person. **True**. Holding a grudge is like taking poison a little at a time to harm the other person. This harms only oneself.

5. False. Negative thoughts and feelings about a person mean I still have a grudge. **False**. Forgiveness is in the *will*, not in the mind or in the emotions. If I will (decide) to forgive the person, then I have forgiven that person.

c. *Obstacles to healing* (continued) - *t/f Quiz*

6 ◯ Forgiving a person means trusting that person.

7 ◯ You cannot make a person love you
(or love you more).

8 ◯ Loving increases stress.

9 ◯ The emotion of hate is the opposite of love.

10 ◯ To forgive is easier than many people think it is.

6. False. Forgiving a person means trusting that person. **False**. One can forgive a person and still mistrust that person. Once a person loses trust in another, that other person must earn, regain, that trust.

7. True. You cannot make a person love you (or love you more). **True**. Loving is a free choice from the will. The door of the heart to love opens only from the inside.

8. True. Loving increases stress. **True**. For many reasons.

9. False. The emotion of hate is the opposite of love. **False**. Love is a Commitment that includes a set of positive, beneficial, decisions to be carried out over a long period of time; e.g., marriage and parenting. A Commitment to hate is rare. The opposite of the *emotion* of love is the feeling of apathy, indifference.

10. True. To forgive is easier than many people think it is. **True**. Forgiveness is in the *will*, not in the mind or in the emotions. Once you *will, decide,* to forgive, you have forgiven even though negative thoughts and feelings return from time to time. Just ignore negative thoughts and negative feelings. *Do not focus on them.*
Refer to the notes on forgiveness. (pages 48, 49, 50)

d. The art of forgiveness

Forgiveness is NOT

In the mind and thoughts or in the emotions and feelings.

Forgiveness IS

In the will.

If I will to forgive, then I have forgiven, even if I have negative thoughts and negative feelings. Just ignore these negative thoughts and negative feelings.

Forgiving means:
- No retaliation or revenge
- Saying some prayers for the person
- Giving help when required
  or requested (if there is no danger to self)

Seeking forgiveness includes:
   - Asking God for forgiveness
   - Asking the person for forgiveness
   - Making compensation if needed.

If the person refuses to forgive you, leave the matter in God's hands. You have done your part-be at peace.

e. The radiance of forgiveness

If I refuse to forgive someone, my inner peace will suffocate under the quicksand of resentment and grudges.

Forgiveness does not come from my feelings. Forgiveness does not come from my mind. Forgiveness comes from my will.

Once I have freely chosen to forgive someone by a decision of my will, the negative feelings and critical thoughts I have do not matter.

I will allow these natural negative feelings and critical thoughts to come and go.

Forgiving a person will open up my mind, heart, and spirit for receiving love from others.

The way of forgiveness leads me to healing and peace within.

f. The radiance of acceptance

Resistance to reality results in turmoil.

Complete acceptance of flaws and faults in myself and in others lays the foundation of peace within necessary for improving self and for strengthening relationships.

Because the behavior of others are beyond my control, I will stop trying to change other people.

Because I do not have access to the depths of a person's emotional life or subconscious, I will accept and respect people without trying to understand them better.

Because love cannot be forced but must be freely given, I will accept the fact that I cannot make a person love me, or love me more.

Because I cannot make others happy, I will create a loving atmosphere wherein others can be happy if they choose to be happy.

$\mathcal{F}$. Living in Radiance

a. APT living for radiance

- **Acceptance** of my present situation with
- **Purpose** in mind for doing well the
- **Task** at hand

APT will create the aptitude for:
- doing quality work
- relating well with others
- enjoying my life more fully

I will be like the wise sailor of a sail boat in choppy seas, who makes full use of all that is within his control, instead of focusing on the forces of the wind and waves that are beyond his control.

Because everything I do affects and forms my thoughts, feelings, and character, I will focus on fulfilling my daily tasks well, and with inner calmness.

I will shape and transform myself into a patient, reliable, loving person through APT living.

b. *The small steps to radiance*

"Heal" comes from the Greek root "kailo" and the angle-Saxon root "hal", which are also the roots for "healthy", whole" and "holy".

These are the small steps to being healed, healthy, whole, holy.

Daily Reminders
- All my negative emotions are good, beneficial.
- All my stress is good, beneficial.
- I can improve all my relationships, even the worst one.
- I will allow God within me to heal me from within.

Daily Behavior
- I will accept all negative emotions in myself and in others.
- I will use stress as motivating energy for helping others and myself.
- I will do centering prayer at least twice a day to let God heal me from within.

Daily Therapy

I will use the relaxation technique nightly before bed:
- to dissolve the residual effects of daily stress
- to get a better night's rest for a fresh start the next morning
- to allow my brain, nervous system, emotions, and body to repair themselves during sleep
- to let God heal me from within during sleep.

I will use APT living:
- **A**cceptance of every situation for the
- **P**urpose of helping others and myself by doing well the
- **T**ask at hand here and now.

c. The journey to radiance (map)

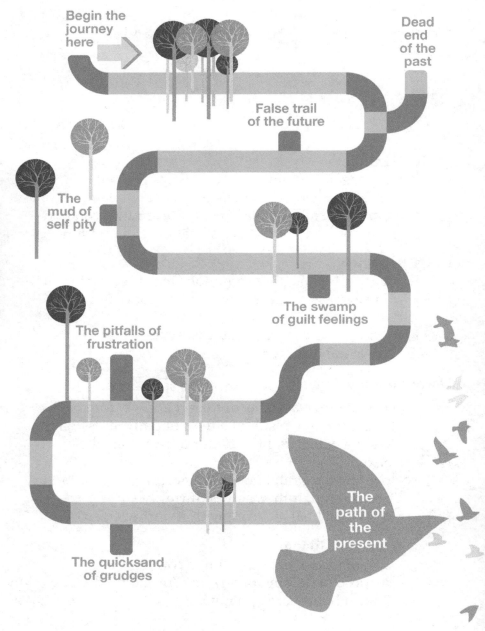

Begin the journey here

Dead end of the past

False trail of the future

The mud of self pity

The swamp of guilt feelings

The pitfalls of frustration

The path of the present

The quicksand of grudges

Take a Break

Three men died during the Christmas season.
Their souls appear before St. Peter at the Gate of Heaven.

St. Peter:
"If you have something in your pocket on earth that
you can connect to Christmas, I will let you into Heaven."

Man #1:
I have a cigarette lighter in my pocket.
You can use the lighter to light Christmas candles."

St. Peter:
"Good; welcome to Heaven."

Man #2:
 I have some keys in my pocket.
They tinkle like Christmas bells."

St. Peter:
"Good; welcome
to Heaven."

Man #3:
"I have a lady's panties
in my pocket."
This man also entered
Heaven. How did he
connect the lady's
panties to Christmas
to enter Heaven?

The Cracked Jar
(A true story)

A handsome college athlete was one of the most popular men on the basketball team. Because of bone cancer, they amputated his right leg above the knee. He refused to return to school, drank heavily, used drugs, and had several auto accidents. His former coach intervened and referred him to a psychiatrist.

He was full of rage and self-pity at the injustice of his plight. When the psychiatrist asked him to draw a picture of his body, he drew the outline of a jar with a large crack running down the entire length of the jar: his body was broken and no longer able to perform as it used to. His anger began to subside. Then he brought in articles about people severely injured by accidents: a man who lost his leg in a motorcycle accident, a girl badly burnt in a house fire, a boy who lost his hand in the explosion of his chemistry set. He made harsh judgments against the doctors and parents for not healing them psychologically. Then he asked if he could meet with some of these patients. The doctor arranged it and in a few weeks he began meeting some of these patients.

He came back from these visits with delight that he could reach them and help some of them. His favorite story was about a twenty-one-year old girl who had both her breasts removed

because her mother, two sisters, and a cousin all had breast cancer. He visited her on a hot summer day and was wearing shorts, so his artificial leg was in full view. Deeply depressed, she lay on her bed with eyes closed, refusing to look at him. He tried everything he knew to reach her, but without success. He made jokes, and even got angry. She did not respond. Frustrated, he unstrapped his artificial leg and thumped it on the floor.
The noise startled her; she opened her eyes and

saw him for the first time. He began hopping around the room and snapping his fingers in time to the soft rock music from her radio and laughing out loud. She burst out laughing and said, "Fella, if you can dance, maybe I can sing."

Then they both began visiting people in the hospital. She was in college and encouraged him to return to college for a degree in psychology to carry his work further. Eventually she became his wife, who was very different from the cheerleaders and models he used to date.

At our last session I showed him the picture he had drawn of the broken jar. He looked at it for some time. Then he said, "It's really not finished." Taking a yellow crayon, he drew thick yellow lines radiating from the crack to all the edges of the paper. He put his finger on the crack, looked at me, and said softly, "This is where the light comes through."

The crack in the heart or the soul is where the light comes through.

· ·

Answer to question:
How did the third man connect the lady's panties to Christmas to enter Heaven? He told St. Peter, "They're Carol's".

After-thought: "Who's Carol?"

"She's my wife."

"Okay, then. Welcome to Heaven."

Part II

Radiance in Turmoil

Relaxation is relative. If we are 100% relaxed, we would be dead. The most relaxed state we can achieve is to be physically relaxed and using only one sense or faculty in a minimal way.

Prelude: Peace Within

The calmness of a lake cannot be found outside the lake.

Personal peace cannot be found outside oneself.

I can find personal peace only within myself.

Sometimes I cannot experience inner peace even when I'm alone in a peaceful place.

The deep peace within myself eludes me.

A lake's calmness is most profound at its deepest depth.

I will find the most profound peace deep within the center of my soul.

Overview

Part II
Radiance in Turmoil

Personal peace cannot be found outside oneself.

$\mathcal{A}$. The Radiance Within

a. Where am I?

Why am I so restless?

Why do I feel so troubled or anxious?

How can I find and experience the peace that is within me?

What is blocking the path to peace within? Is it my work?
Other people? Myself?

Beside Myself?
Most of the time I feel wound up or stressed out.
    - I have too many things to do.
    - Others expect too much of me.
    - My schedule is too hectic
    - I'm feeling too pressured

b. The radiance of stress

The stress in my life is like:
- the engine in my car
- the wind in my sail
- the colors in my favorite painting
- the rhythm in my favorite music
- the love I have for others

*I can transform the stress in
my life into a source of benefits.*

I will respect and accept the stress in my life.

I will view it as a challenge.

I will use it as part of my commitment to my family.

I will enjoy stress as part of my personal/professional development.

c. Radiance within

My body-mind has the innate ability to maintain health
and to heal itself.

My brain is its own designer, engineer, chemist, and healer.
My brain is continually remaking and renewing itself.

Complete relaxation allows my brain to heal and renew itself.

I will use relaxation techniques for inner healing
and daily renewal.

When really slowed down, my heart has been designed
for healing the damages of persistent stress.

I will use slow deep breathing to slow down my heart rate.

*I will calm my mind, emotions, and heart, so
my brain and body will heal themselves of the
harmful effects of persistent stress, and restore
wellness within.*

My daily calming of mind, emotions, and heart will relieve
stress and maintain a healthy balance.

I will use relaxation techniques so my ingrained wellness
will spring up and flow into my mind, emotions, and body,
for healing and for enjoying life more fully.

d. Calming my inner self

Relaxing your body, sit comfortably with a straight back to balance your head, and then do deep breathing (abdominal breathing) in this manner:

> I will inhale slowly from the bottom of my lungs upward for a full but relaxed breath, pause briefly, and then exhale slowly.
> - While inhaling slowly, I mentally count one;
> - While exhaling slowly, I mentally count one.
> - When I reach ten, I will begin another
>   set of ten relaxed breaths.

Doing three, five, or more of these sets of ten breaths will:
- dissolve tension
- lower my blood pressure
- and allow inner healing to refresh my body,
  mind, heart, and spirit

e. Steps into radiance

1. Relaxing my body

Raise your arms straight up with palms facing frontward, and then stretch upward on tiptoes as high as you can.

Do this three times.

1. With your arms hanging as limp as wet towels, swing your arms left and right by twisting your hips and torso left and right. Do seven to ten sets of this.

2. Gently and slowly lower your head forward as far down as it will go, as if to touch your collarbone with your chin. Hold for five seconds.

3. Gently and slowly pull your head backward as far back as it will go. Hold for five seconds. Repeat this forward and backward stretching of your neck muscles three times.

4. With shoulders relaxed and arms hanging limp, rotate your head slowly in wide smooth circles seven to ten times. Then do the same thing in the opposite direction.

5. With shoulders relaxed and arms hanging limp, slowly rotate your shoulders forward in wide smooth circles seven to ten times. Do the same thing with a backward rotation.

2. A regular nightly practice

I will relax my body and calm my inner self nightly
to dissolve the accumulated stress of the day:
- to fall asleep peacefully,
- to get a better night's rest,
- to wake up more refreshed.

Just before getting into bed, I will use
the relaxation technique to relax my body.

After getting into bed, I will use slow deep breathing
to calm my inner self.

I will do this complete relaxation technique every night
as my first major step on the path to peace within.

3. My daily application

   Whenever I'm wound up or anxious
   - at home, at work, or elsewhere.

   - I will use the following slow deep
     breathing technique:

        As I inhale slowly and deeply,
        mentally I say, "I breathe in peace;"

        As I exhale slowly,
        mentally I say, "I breathe out stress."

           Or

        As I inhale slowly and deeply,
        mentally I say, "I breathe in calmness;"

        As I exhale slowly,
        mentally I say, "I breathe out tension."

   After doing this for two or three minutes,
   I will be calm, clear, and centered.

I will
be calm,
clear and
centered.

a. The darkness of the past

The past events of my life no longer exist. They're gone.

I bear the residual effects of my past, but I will not allow the stress of my past to seep into my present situations.

After complete acceptance of past pain and suffering, there is no need for me to focus on the pain of the past.

Focusing on the distress or pain of the past only contaminates my present situations.

I will empty my mind and heart of the bad or painful events of my past through relaxation techniques or exercise.

I will ignore and deflect feelings and reactions from the past by focusing completely on the present task at hand.

I will attend to the present.

b. The false path of the future

The future does not actually exist. It may exist in my mind or imagination only as thoughts or imaginings.

Because worry changes nothing,
Worrying about the future will
not change my future.

The best preparation for my future is to deal well with the present.

I will give my full attention to the present tasks at hand.

c. The dark mud of self-pity

Focusing on:
- my bad luck
- my mistakes
- mistreatment from others
- injustices suffered
- will lead me to self-pity.

Seeking pity by telling others about my struggles and misfortunes will lead me to self-pity.

I will never find inner peace in the mud of self-pity.

I will focus on the positive aspects of my life.

I will talk about the positive aspects of my life.

I will give my full attention to the present tasks at hand.

d. The dark swamp of guilt feelings

Guilt feelings will block out the experience of inner peace.

"I cannot forgive "myself" really means,
I will not let go of my guilt feelings."

After seeking forgiveness from the person I have offended or hurt, I may still feel guilty, but I will no longer be guilty.

So I will let go of my guilt feelings by refusing to give them my attention.

I will drop my feelings of guilt by refusing to recall my failings, by refusing to focus on my mistakes.

When feelings of guilt return, I will turn my attention to my present tasks at hand.

I can change what I'm feeling by focusing my attention on something else, or by doing something else.

e. The dark pit of frustrations

The most common source of frustration is trying to control things that are beyond my control.

Trying to control what's beyond my control:
- frustrates me
- stresses me out
- wastes my time
- drains my energy
- gives me a sense of helplessness.

I will learn to accept or ignore the things that are beyond my control, (such as other people's behavior, the weather, the situation in our country or elsewhere).

With practice I will gain control over my:

External senses
— sight, hearing, touch, taste, smell.

Inner faculties
— simple reasoning, memory, imagination, and emotions.

Spiritual powers
— intellect and free will.

With this control I can prevent a lot of frustration.

With this control I can choose my reactions and responses to people, events, and things, and thus preserve my peace within.

f. Dealing with frustrations

The greatest source of frustration for 99% of us is trying to control what is beyond our control.

This is so frustrating because we are trying to do the impossible.

When frustrated, ask "Is this within my control?" If not, then just accept the situation and drop the matter.

If it is within your control, improve the part that is within your control.

Frustrations are part of human living and relationships. We have no control over: the laws of nature, such as weather, causes of disease or what others think, say and do.

The only control we have is over our responses: what we decide to think, feel, do.

We can influence what we think, feel, and do by focusing our attention. By changing what we focus on, we can change our thoughts, feelings, and even our behavior.

Try focusing on something that will bring laughter - what are your thoughts and feelings?

Try focusing on something that makes you sad, sorrowful - what are your thoughts and feelings?

You now know how to lessen the frustrations in your life.

g. The radiance of the present

The stress and pressure of the present exist mainly in my mind, imagination, and emotions.

The present moment is small and manageable.

The flow of time is nature's way of preventing everything from happening all at once.

I will take a deep breath, pause briefly, then expel the stress and pressure of the present with my outgoing breath.

Then I will focus on my present task at hand.

Doing my present task one step at a time makes every task manageable.

In the emergency room, a doctor treating a severely injured person with excessive bleeding works only one step at a time.

When working one step at a time, any stress experienced helps rather than hinders.

When I am totally present psychologically and spiritually, I generate greater energy and power.

Because I cannot change another person, to strengthen a relationship I will focus on changing myself.

𝒞. Radiance for Others

a. The radiance of acceptance

Resistance to reality results in turmoil.

Complete acceptance of flaws and faults in myself and in others, lays the foundation of peace within, necessary for improving myself, and for strengthening my relationships.

Because the behavior of others are beyond my control, I will stop trying to change other people.

> *Because I do not have access to the depths of a person's emotional life or subconscious, I will accept and respect people without trying to understand them better.*

Because love cannot be forced but must be freely given, I will accept the fact that I cannot make a person love me, or love me more.

Because I cannot make others happy: I will create a loving atmosphere wherein others can be happy, if they choose to be happy.

b. The darkness of grudges

Holding a grudge against someone is like throwing stones at him while I'm sinking in quicksand a little at a time; the stones miss him while I'm sinking.

The more I focus on a grudge, the more I sink into the quicksand of suffocation.

Because grudges destroy my inner peace, I will let go of them to preserve my peace within.

Grudges prevent the free flow of emotions throughout my body-mind — a flow necessary for inner healing.

Letting go of grudges by focusing my attention on the positive aspects of my life will also set others at peace.

c. The radiance of forgiveness

If I refuse to forgive someone, my inner peace will suffocate under the quicksand of resentment and grudges.

Forgiveness does not come from my feelings.
Forgiveness does not come from my mind.
Forgiveness comes from my will.

Once I have freely chosen to forgive someone by a decision of my will, the negative feelings and critical thoughts I have do not matter.

I will allow these natural negative feelings and critical thoughts to come and go.

Forgiving a person will open up my mind, heart, and spirit for receiving love from others.

The way of forgiveness leads me to peace within.

d. The radiance of love

> *The more I love others:*
> *   - the more I worry about them*
> *   - the more I suffer with them when they suffer*
> *   - the more I sacrifice for them*
> *   - the more vulnerable I become*
> *   - the more sensitive I become.*

I will accept the negative emotions of anger, disappointment, and frustration that come with loving.

I will accept the negative thoughts and judgments that come with loving.

Loving brings me lower lows, but also higher highs.

Loving divides my sorrows, and doubles my joys.

e. The radiance of peace

Because I cannot change another person, to improve
our relationship I will focus on changing myself.

To improve any of my relationships,
I have to change myself:
    - my expectations
    - my reactions and responses
    - my attitudes
    - my words and actions.

Accepting others without pressuring them to
change sets me at peace, and sets them at peace.

Because nagging begets resentment and resistance,
I will limit the number of my kindly reminders.
Preserving my peace within will make me easier
to work with, and easier to live with.

Peace.

a. Healing laughter

Because a healthy sense of humor is essential for mental, emotional, and spiritual health, and for loving, I will give greater importance to humor and laughter.

Because deep laughter dissolves stress, and lessens pain and depression instantly, I will use laughter to soothe stress and loosen up.

Because carefree laughter prepares me to deal with challenges, and to give and receive love, I will try to see the humorous side of serious situations.

Because laughter heals and strengthens me psychologically and spiritually, I will allow myself more carefree laughter.

b. Creative laughter

The "Ha, ha, ha," of laughter is connected to the "Ah ha!" of discovery.

Because laughter can open and prepare my mind for a new insight, I will use humor and laughter to be more creative.

Because humor and laughter can help me to see and interpret things in a different and new way, I will use humor and laugher to enhance my creativity.

Because humor and laughter involve the activity of my right brain, I will use humor and laughter to develop my intuitive reasoning.

Because humor and laughter shape and affect my attitudes, I will use humor and laughter to become more loving.

c. Bonding laughter

Because humorous incidents can bring me closer to others, I will take part in group laughter.

Because humor and laughter create a warm and safe atmosphere for living and working, I will encourage the use of humor and laughter.

Because laughter strengthens family bonds, I will promote laughter in my home and family.

Because healthy humor is non-threatening, I will "disarm" myself by making fun of myself.

Because laughing together deepens love, I will learn to laugh more with those I love.

d. The radiance of music

Because relaxing music can lower my heartbeat, pulse rate, and blood pressure, I will use such music to relax my body.

Because music can change my experience of time, foster endurance, and create a sense of well-being, I will use music for my mental and emotional health.

Because music can improve learning, boost mental functioning, and stimulate creativity, I will learn more about the power of music for using it in my life.

Because the power of music has been used for thousands of years to soothe the soul, I will use this power of soothing music for my soul and spirit, and for better relationships.

e. Healing music

Because music has been used to heal disorders and diseases in China and India for many centuries, I will learn about the healing power of music for myself and for others.

Because music can reduce muscle tension, improve body movement and coordination, and increase endorphin levels, I will use relaxing music for dissolving stress and for enjoyment.

Because lively tunes and upbeat music can lift me up from my feelings of anxiety and depression, I will raise my spirits with lively, upbeat music.

Because of its clarity, elegance, and vitality, I will use classical music to heal my soul and spirit.

f. Inspiring music

Because the music of marching bands and powerful symphonies can stir up my emotions and move me to action, I will use it when there's a need for it.

Because Spirituals, Gospel and sacred music can lift my spirits and deepen my faith, I will use religious music to help me to pray.

Because I need inner stillness for contemplative prayer, I will use soothing religious music for inner stillness.

Because romantic music is so expressive and sensual, I will use it to enhance sympathy and love.

Take a Break

What does a dog do that a man steps into? (not poop).
Answer: pants.

••

A couple married for nearly 40 years were retired, sitting on the
porch and enjoying a glass of wine while ending the day.

The wife says, "I don't know how I would ever live without you."

The husband asks, "Is that you talking or the wine talking?"
How did the wife reply?

••

A visitor saw three men in Chartres who were cutting
stone to help build the Cathedral. He asked each man what
he was doing.

The first man said, "I'm cutting stone blocks 12"x12"x12".
I've been doing this for three years, and will keep doing
this as long as I can."

The second man said, "I'm cutting stone blocks 12"x12"x12"
to support my wife and three children. With this work I'm
able to provide them with food, clothing, and a loving home.

The third man said, "I'm helping to build a
grand Cathedral. This sacred place will be a
light of faith for many people for centuries.

How did the wife reply?
She said, "It's me talking; to the wine!"

• •

A woman living alone on Social Security was lonely. She passed by a pet shop with the sign: "Talking parrot for sale – regular $300, on sale for $50."

Even on sale the parrot would be a stretch on her budget.

"Does the parrot really talk? I need company."

"Sally is guaranteed to talk. Give her two weeks to adjust."

She takes the parrot home. For two weeks not a word. Finally on the 15th day Sally says, "Hi, I'm Sally the swinger and I sleep around a lot." That's all she repeats. Imagine her embarrassment when her church friends come to visit and Sally keeps repeating, "Hi, I'm Sally the swinger and I sleep around a lot."

She couldn't return a sale item and couldn't kill Sally.

"I'll take it to the pastor. He'll know what to do. He has two parrots."

When she brings Sally to the pastor and explains her problem, he says, "Don't worry. I have two parrots, Herbie and Danny. I taught them the 'Hail Mary'. Herbie says 'Hail Mary, Hail Mary' and Danny says 'Pray for us, Pray for us'.

I'll put Sally in with Herbie and Danny and she'll learn to pray."

For two weeks not a word. Then Sally says, "Hi, I'm Sally the swinger and I sleep around a lot."

Herbie looks at Danny and says "Our prayers have been answered!!!"

After-thought: If God will answer the prayers of parrots, you can be sure God will answer the prayers of His dear children. Miracles are very, very, very rare, because usually God allows two limitations to the power of prayer:

1) the laws of nature in physics, chemistry and biology.

2) the use of free will
   (God never interferes with free will or free choices.)

Ravensbruck was a Nazi concentration camp about 50 miles north of Berlin for Jewish woman and children. More than 150,000 persons were killed there.

An unknown woman wrote this note and pinned it to the dead body of a little girl: "O Lord, remember not only the men and women of good will, but also those of ill will. But do not remember all the sufferings they have inflicted on us. Remember rather the fruits we have bought, thanks to this suffering: our comradeship, our loyalty, our humility, our courage, our generosity; the greatness of heart which has grown out of all this. And when they come to judgment, let all the fruits which we have borne be their forgiveness."

Radiance of Loving

Although I am a sensual-emotional person, I am primarily a willful, purposeful, and creative person.

Prelude: The Journey of Loving

My loving is nourished within my stream of daily living,
and flows out of my stream of daily living.

In living well and in loving well,
I can and must:
        - exercise control,
        - make decisions,
        - and choose wisely.
Both require patience, endurance,
and perseverance.

Our society tries to make doing things easy and fast;
but learning to love is difficult and takes a long time.

Love cannot grow or survive in the midst of inner turmoil.

The personal peace I need for loving can be found only inside
myself. I will find the most profound peace deep within the
center of my soul. True lasting love comes from the deepest
depth of my soul.

Overview

Part III
Radiance of Loving

$\mathcal{A}$. The Radiance of Loving

a. The challenge of loving

Why am I fearful in my relationships?

Why do I feel so troubled or anxious?

How can I find and experience the peace that nourishes my loving?

What is blocking my path to better relationships? Is it my work? Other people? Myself? Others? Others expect too much of me.

I'm feeling pressured by people.

The stress of loving is like:
  - *the engine in my car*
  - *the wind in my sail*
  - *the colors in my favorite painting*
  - *the rhythm in my favorite music*
  - *the warmth of love I feel for others.*

I can transform this stress into a source of benefits for others and for myself.

I will view this stress as a challenge for becoming a better person.

I will use the stress of loving as part of my commitment to those I love.

b. The stress of loving

The more I love others:
- the more I worry about them
- the more I suffer with them when they suffer
- the more I sacrifice for them
- the more vulnerable I become
- the more sensitive I become.

I will accept the negative emotions of anger, disappointment, and frustration that come with loving.

I will accept the negative thoughts and judgments that come with loving.

Loving brings me lower lows, but also higher highs.

Loving divides my sorrows,
and doubles my joys.

It is the same sensitivity whereby I both love and suffer.

The more loving I am, the deeper the suffering.

My heart aches so much because I am such a loving person.

I will use relaxation techniques daily to deal well with the stress of roving, to strengthen my relationships.

c. The breath of living and loving

Arab proverb:

"Life is in the breath.
He who half breathes, half lives."

We can add: He who half lives, half loves.

Shallow breathing limits my capabilities.

Deep breathing accesses my full potential.

I will use slow deep breathing:
- to gain control of my mind and body
- to be more aware
- to develop the wisdom of my body and my emotions.

My slow deep breathing will join brain, body, mind, heart, and spirit for unified effectiveness.

My slow deep breathing will strengthen the force and flow of my inner energy.

My slow deep breathing will balance the physical-emotional-mental-spiritual energy within.

d. Born to love

Because our brain and nervous system are hardwired for loving, few things are as universal as humans loving.

When really slowed down, my mind, heart, and spirit, have been designed for recovering from the stress of loving.

My daily calming of mind, emotions, and heart will relieve stress, and maintain a healthy balance.

I will use relaxation techniques so my innate ability to love will grow and develop.

e. Day by day

Whenever I'm wound up or anxious at home, at work, or elsewhere, I will use the following slow deep breathing technique:

As I inhale slowly and deeply, mentally I say,
"I breathe in peace;"

As I exhale slowly, mentally I say,
"I breathe out stress."

Or

As I inhale slowly and deeply, mentally I say,
"I breathe in calmness;"

As I exhale slowly, mentally I say,
"I breathe out tension."

Or

As I inhale slowly and deeply, mentally I say,
"I breathe in love;"

As I exhale slowly, mentally I say,
"I breathe out peace."

Human Living

Human living consists in a continual series of:

Responses

Internal
- thoughts
- decisions
- emotions

External
- words
- body language
- actions

To

God
Self
Others
Things

A commitment is a big complex decision that includes a set of many decisions to be carried out over a long period of time.

Human Loving

Human loving consists in a series of:

Responses

Internal
- positive commitment
- positive decisions
- positive attitudes
- positive or negative judgments
- positive or negative emotions

External
- beneficial words
- beneficial body language
- beneficial actions

To

The person loved

There is no need for me to focus on the pain of the past. Focusing on the distress or pain of the past only contaminates my present relationships.

f. Relaxing my body

Raise your arms straight up with palms facing frontward, and then stretch upward on tiptoes as high as you can.

Do this three times.

1. With your arms hanging as limp as wet towels, swing your arms left and right by twisting your hips and torso left and right. Do seven to ten sets of this.

2. Gently and slowly lower your head forward as far down as it will go, as if to touch your collarbone with your chin. Hold for five seconds.

3. Gently and slowly pull your head backward as far back as it will go. Hold for five seconds. Repeat this forward and backward stretching of your neck muscles three times.

4. With shoulders relaxed and arms hanging limp, rotate your head slowly in wide smooth circles seven to ten times. Then do the same thing in the opposite direction.

5. With shoulders relaxed and arms hanging limp, slowly rotate your shoulders forward in wide smooth circles seven to ten times. Do the same thing with a backward rotation.

g. Calming my inner self

Relaxing your body, sit comfortably with a straight back to balance your head, and then do deep breathing (abdominal breathing) in this manner:

I will inhale slowly from the bottom of my lungs upward for a full but relaxed breath, pause briefly, then exhale slowly.

- While inhaling slowly, I mentally count one.
- While exhaling slowly, I mentally count one.
- When I reach ten, I will begin another set of ten relaxed breaths.

Doing three, five, or more of these sets of ten breaths will:
- dissolve tension,
- lower my blood pressure,
- and allow inner healing
- to refresh my body, mind, heart, and spirit.

h. A regular nightly practice

I will relax my body and calm my inner self nightly
to dissolve the accumulated stress of the day:
- to fall asleep peacefully,
- to get a better night's rest,
- to wake up more refreshed.

Just before getting into bed, I will use the relaxation
technique to relax my body.

After getting into bed, I will use slow deep breathing
to calm my inner self.

I will do this complete relaxation technique every night
as my first major step on the path to peace within.

i. Directing the inner flow

Although I am a sensual-emotional person, I am primarily a willful, purposeful, and creative person.

I can direct the flow of my emotions by: focusing my attention on this or that, talking about this or that, or doing this or that.

> *I will gain greater control over my emotions by directing the use of my:*
> - *external senses*
>   - *— sight, hearing, smell, touch, taste*
> - *inner faculties*
>   - *— simple reasoning, memory, imagination, emotions*
> - *spiritual powers*
>   - *— intellect and free will to enhance my ability to love.*

I will learn to direct the flow of my emotions to preserve the peace within me, that nourishes my loving.

I will use the relaxation technique of slow deep breathing to calm the commotion within, for better communication and relationships.

*I will
dare
to love
again.*

$\mathcal{B}$. The Path to Loving

a. The dead weight of the past

The past events of my life no longer exist.

They're gone.

I will empty my mind and heart of the bad or painful events of my past.

I bear the residual effects of my past, but I will not allow the struggles of my past to seep into my present relationships.

There is no need for me to focus on the pain of the past. Focusing on the distress or pain of the past only contaminates my present relationships.

I will focus on the present. Because past events no longer exist, I will love as if I have never been hurt before.

b. The mirage of the future

The future does not actually exist. It may exist in my mind or imagination only as thoughts or imaginings.

Because worry changes nothing, worrying about the future in a relationship will not change that relationship in any way. Worrying about the future drains away my energy, and add unnecessary stress to my present relationships.

The best preparation for my future is to deal well with my present.

I will give my full attention to the present tasks at hand. Because scar tissue is twice as tough, I will dare to love again.

c. The slush of self-pity

Focusing on:
- my bad luck
- my mistakes
- mistreatment from others
- injustices suffered
- will lead me to self-pity.

Seeking pity by telling others about my struggles and misfortunes will lead me to self-pity.

The slush of self-pity impedes my relationships.

I will focus on the positive aspects of my life.

I will talk about the positive aspects of my life.

I will give my full attention to the present tasks at hand to better my relationships.

Because I can choose my responses and behavior, I will allow myself to be loved.

Because my soul is beautiful, and my spirit is a thing of beauty, I am loved.

d. The potholes of frustration

The most common source of frustration is trying to control the behavior of others, which is beyond my control.

Trying to control what's beyond my control:
- frustrates me
- stresses me out
- wastes my time
- drains my energy
- gives me a sense of helplessness.

I will learn to accept or ignore the things that are beyond my control (such as other people's behavior, the weather, the situation in our country or elsewhere).

With practice I will gain control over my:

external senses
— sight, hearing, touch, taste, smell

inner faculties
— simple reasoning, memory, imagination, emotions

spiritual powers
— intellect and free will.

With this control I can prevent a lot of frustration.

With this control I can choose my reactions and responses to people, events, and things, and thus preserve my peace within, and build good relationships.

e. Dealing with frustrations

The greatest source of frustration for 99% of us is trying to control what is beyond our control. This is so frustrating because we are trying to do the impossible.

When frustrated, ask "Is this within my control?" If not, then just accept the situation and drop the matter. If it is within your control, improve the part that is within your control.

Frustrations are part of human living and relationships.

We have no control over: the laws of nature, such as weather, causes of disease, what others think, say and do.

The only control we have is over our responses: what we decide to think, feel, do.

We can influence what we think, feel, and do by focusing our attention.

By changing what we focus on, we can change:
   - our thoughts, feelings,
   - and even our behavior.

Try focusing on something that will bring laughter - what are your thoughts and feelings? Try focusing on something that makes you sad, sorrowful – what are your thoughts and feelings.

You now know how to lessen the frustrations in your life.

f. The dark muck of guilt feelings

Guilt feelings will block out the experience of inner peace, and hinder my relationships.

"I cannot forgive myself" really means,
"I will not let go of my guilt feelings."

After seeking forgiveness from the person I have offended or hurt, I will let go of my guilt feelings.

I will drop my feelings of guilt by refusing to recall my failings, by refusing to focus on my mistakes.

When feelings of guilt return, I will turn my attention to my present tasks at hand.

I can change what I'm feeling by focusing my attention on something else.

g. The simple path of the present

The stress and pressure of relationships exist mainly in my mind, imagination, and emotions.

The present moment is small and manageable.

The flow of time is nature's way of preventing everything from happening all at once.

I will take a deep breath, pause briefly, then expel the stress and pressure of the present with my outgoing breath.

Then I will focus on my present task at hand.

Doing my present task one step at a time makes every task manageable.

In the emergency room, a doctor treating a severely injured person with excessive bleeding works only one step at a time.

When working one step at a time, any stress experienced helps rather than hinders.

h. Dealing with negative emotions

Because all emotions are good, I will learn to accept the negative emotions of others without becoming defensive, especially with loved ones.

I will learn to deflect criticisms or harsh words directed at me by not taking them in a personal way, especially from loved ones.

> *I will not descend to the muck of retaliation when I am offended or hurt by someone, especially by a loved one.*

I will secretly calm myself with slow deep breathing when someone angry or upset confronts me, especially someone I love.

i. Dealing with conflicts

Because conflicts are a part of loving and can strengthen love, I will accept conflicts and resolve them without casting blame.

Because I cannot change another person, to improve our relationship I will focus on changing myself.

To improve any of my relationships,
I have to change myself:
- my expectations
- my reactions and responses
- my attitudes
- my words and actions

Accepting others without pressuring them to change sets me at peace, and sets them at peace.

Because nagging begets resentment and resistance, I will limit the number of my kindly reminders.

Preserving my peace within will make me easier to work with, easier to live with, more loving to others.

To build a strong relationship, the "bricks" of shared activity that I use must be of sufficient quantity and quality.

j. The darkness of grudges

Holding a grudge against someone is like trying to kill him by taking poison a little at a time — it kills me instead without harming him.

The more I focus on a grudge, the more I sink into the quicksand of suffocation, which stifles love.

Because grudges destroy my inner peace, I will let go of them and preserve my inner peace, that nourishes my loving.

Letting go of grudges by focusing my attention on the positive aspects of my life will also set others at peace.

I will let go of resentment toward my loved ones by focusing my attention on their positive traits, and their acts of kindness.

C. Family, Friends and Foes

a. The radiance of acceptance

What is, *is*; *what happens,* happens.

Accept and work with what is.

Because the behavior of others is beyond my control, I will stop trying to change the people I love.

Because I do not have access to the depths of a person's emotional life or subconscious, I will accept my loved ones even if I don't understand them fully.

Because I cannot make others happy, I will create a loving atmosphere wherein others can be happy if they choose to be happy.

b. The radiance of forgiveness

For if you forgive men their trespasses, your heavenly Father also will forgive you. Mt 6:14

If I refuse to forgive someone, my inner peace will suffocate under the quicksand of resentment and grudges.

- Forgiveness does not come from my feelings.
- Forgiveness does not come from my mind.
- Forgiveness comes from my will.

Once I have freely chosen to forgive someone by a decision of my will, the negative feelings and critical thoughts I have do not matter.

I will allow these natural negative feelings and critical thoughts to come and go.

Forgiving a person will open up my mind, heart, and spirit for receiving love from others.

The way of forgiveness leads me to peace within.

c. Inner peace

I will transform daily stress into a power-source for my commitments to my loved ones, and to the challenges of my own growth and development.

With my regular nightly practice of relaxing my body and calming my inner self, I will be still enough to experience my inner peace, and better prepared for being loving the next day.

With my daily use of the slow deep breathing technique, I will be calm, clear, and centered for relating well with others.

I will use relaxation techniques daily to calm my mind, emotions, and heart, to experience the peace deep with me, and to let my love flow from the depths of my soul.

I will drop my feelings of guilt by refusing to recall my failings, by refusing to focus on my mistakes.

$\mathcal{D}$. The Practice of Loving

a. Self-giving

Because selfishness stunts my ability to love, I will work at overcoming selfishness by helping others more often.

Because arrogance weakens my ability to love, I will work at showing greater respect to others, and work at treating others as equals.

Because loving involves the giving of myself, I will gain greater control over myself to improve my ability to love.

Because loving goes beyond my thoughts and feelings, I will rise to the level of will and behavior.

Because loving includes critical thoughts and negative feelings, I will rise above them to the level of supportive words and acts of kindness.

Because loving is a commitment — a big complex decision that includes a set of positive decisions, positive attitudes, and positive behavior over a long period of time - I will accept the hurts, the bad, and the ugly, along with the joy, delight, and fulfillment of loving.

I will use relaxation techniques daily for giving love to others more freely, and for receiving love from others more freely.

b. APT living

In the choppy seas of relationships, I will be a wise sailor of a sail boat who makes full use of all that is within my control, instead of focusing on the forces of wind and waves that are beyond my control.

Because everything I do affects and forms my thoughts, feelings, and character, and my ability to give and receive love, I will focus on fulfilling my daily tasks well and with inner calmness.

> APT living for Loving
> — Acceptance of my present situation with
> — Purpose in mind for doing well the
> — Task at hand - will create the aptitude for:
> - doing quality work,
> - relating well with others,
> - enjoying my life more fully
> - for giving and receiving love.

I will shape and transform myself into a patient, reliable, loving person through APT living.

c. The flow of living and loving

Loving is ongoing and cannot be stored; loving is like staying in shape physically and spiritually.

Because daily changes are continuous in my life, I will flow with these changes like water and work with them, while directing my flow toward my goals.

I will let go of the past and the future to flow with the present, so I can deal with what's real and beneficial.

I will flow around the big rocks in my relationships (things beyond my control) by accepting them or ignoring them.

I will preserve the peace within the center of my soul, the source of my loving, as I flow with changes up and down, side to side.

d. Loving is ....

My loving is not mainly a relationship to a specific person; it is an attitude, an orientation of character, that determines how I relate to every person I know.

My loving is based mainly on my ability to love, which is a basic sensitivity that responds beneficially to what is good and lovable in people.

I will accept and show respect to everyone, to set others at peace, to show them my love.

I will let go of grudges and resentment for internal peace and external peace, to allow my love to flow freely. I will reassure and encourage others with my kind and supportive words to allow my inner peace to flow out to others, as a gift of love to others.

e. The radiance of loving

To develop my ability for loving to its full potential, I will learn and take the path to peace within as essential for loving.

To grow and develop as a loving person, I will labor at the present tasks at hand for the people I care about.

To become a person easier to work with and live with, I will loosen up through daily use of my relaxation techniques, to improve all my relationships.

To dissolve stress and to bond with others, I will laugh more often at myself and use positive humor to become more creative and loving.

f. The circle of faculties

My External Senses of

My Inner Faculties of

My Soul's Powers

My Spirit

of Intellect and Will

Simple Reasoning   Memory   Imagination   Emotions

Sight   Hearing   Touch   Taste   Smell

BODY WITH FIVE EXTERNAL SENSES
Physical Reactions Bodily Activities

An attitude is a pattern of thinking and feeling based on past experiences.

g. A permanent radiance

A stable love relationship is not achieved directly, but can be achieved only as the resulting benefit of:

- mutual communication about the mundane and about values and convictions

- spending time with the person, and spending time for that person

- showing respect to one another verbally and non-verbally.

These three activities are the external activities of loving.

Persons are joined together by thousands of physical-emotional ties, only a few of which are rational and articulable.

The internal activities of loving are positive: commitment + attitudes + judgments + emotions + decisions.

The single most decisive factor in building a permanent love relationship is the quantity and quality of shared activity in daily living.

The single most decisive factor in building a permanent love relationship is the quantity and quality of shared activity in daily living.

Take a Break

What do you get when you cross a porcupine with a turtle?

....

A Catholic couple still deeply in love were celebrating their golden wedding anniversary. Afterward a relative had this conversation with them.

Relative: "Wow! Fifty years of marriage. Didn't you ever have serious problems and doubt about your marriage?"

Husband: "We had lots of problems. Shortly after marriage we were both working to pay the rent and put food on the table."

Wife: "Then the children came and more financial pressure."

Husband: "And we disagreed and argued over the children."

Wife: "We had different values and argued over them."

After they listed some of their other problems, the relative asked, "Didn't you two ever think about divorce?"

Both answered together: "Divorce? No, never! Murder, yes."

Their love commitment carried them through all the lows and problems of marriage.

....

Cross a porcupine with a turtle and you get a slow poke.

At an orphanage for young children, a chubby seven-year-old girl, who was unappealing in face and temperament, was disliked by the other orphans and ignored by the staff. She ate alone and played alone during recess. One day a staff member saw her climb a low tree and put a piece of paper in a cleft. Afterwards the staff member reached up and retrieved the paper. The note was: "Whoever finds this, I love you."

Because God is within me at the center of my soul, I will allow Him to heal me from within.

Prelude to Prayer

Because God is everywhere —
within me at the center of my soul —
I can pray anywhere, anytime.

Because God loves me and cares about me,
He will hear my every prayer.

Because I can talk, I can pray.
Because I can think, I can pray.
Because I can love, I can pray.
I will pray for others and for myself.

Overview

Part IV
Radiance Through Prayer

$\mathcal{A}$. My Inner Journey to God

a. My need for prayer

Take heed, watch and pray. Mark 13:33

Why am I so restless?
Why do I feel so troubled or anxious?
How can I find and experience God within me?

What is blocking my path to God within me?

Is it my work?
Other people?
Myself?

b. My need for God

The Lord is my light and my salvation;
whom should I fear?
The Lord is my life's refuge;
of whom should I be afraid? Psalm 27:1

Sometimes I feel empty inside.
I feel this longing for something unknown.
After a while, I tire of things.
After a while, I tire of people.

"Because You have made us for Thyself, 0 Lord,
our hearts are restless until they rest in Thee."
St. Augustine

c. The breath of life

The Lord God formed man out of dust from the ground, and breathed into his nostrils the breath of life. Gen 2:7

I will use slow deep breathing
to gain control of my mind and body,
as a preparation for prayer.

My slow deep breathing will join
brain, body, heart, and spirit
for a closer union with God.

My slow deep breathing will strengthen
the force and flow of the spiritual energy
that comes from God.

Breathe on us, Breath of God,
until our hearts are pure,
until with You we have one will,
to live and to endure.

Breathe on us, Breath of God,
our souls with grace refine,
until this earthly part of us glows
with fire divine.

Breathe on us, Breath of God,
fill us with life anew, that we may
love the things You love, and do
what You would do.

Breathe on us, Breath of God, so we
shall never die, but give You thanks
and praise throughout eternity.
Amen.

d. The healer within

For I, the Lord, am your healer. Ex 15:26

Because God is within me
at the center of my soul,
I will allow Him to heal me from within.

I will use slow deep breathing
to calm my inner self,
so God can heal me.

I will calm my mind, emotions, and heart,
so God can heal my mind, emotions, and heart
from the wounds of sin and selfishness.

I will use relaxation techniques,
so God's presence within me will be free
to energize me.

*Do you not know that your body is a temple
of the Holy Spirit within you, whom you have
from God, and that you are not your own?
I Cor 6:19*

*Therefore, glorify God in your body.
I Cor 6:20*

e. Relaxing my body

Raise your arms straight up with palms facing frontward, and then stretch upward on tiptoes as high as you can.

Do this three times.

1. With your arms hanging as limp as wet towels, swing your arms left and right by twisting your hips and torso left and right. Do seven to ten sets of this.

2. Gently and slowly lower your head forward as far down as it will go, as if to touch your collarbone with your chin. Hold for five seconds.

3. Gently and slowly pull your head backward as far back as it will go. Hold for five seconds. Repeat this forward and backward stretching of your neck muscles three times.

4. With shoulders relaxed and arms hanging limp, rotate your head slowly in wide smooth circles seven to ten times. Then do the same thing in the opposite direction.

5. With shoulders relaxed and arms hanging limp, slowly rotate your shoulders forward in wide smooth circles seven to ten times. Do the same thing with a backward rotation.

f. Calming my inner self for prayer

*"Quiet! Be still!" The wind ceased
and there was a great calm. Mark 4:39*

Relaxing your body, sit comfortably with a straight back to balance your head, and then do deep breathing (abdominal breathing) in this manner:

I will inhale slowly from the bottom of my lungs upward for a full but relaxed breath, pause briefly, and then exhale slowly.

While inhaling slowly, I mentally count one; while exhaling slowly, I mentally count one.

When I reach ten, I will begin another set of ten relaxed breaths.

Doing three, five, or more of these sets of ten breaths will:

- dissolve tension,
- lower my blood pressure,
- and allow inner healing
- to refresh my body, mind, heart, and spirit,
- prepare me for prayer.

g. *My daily contact with God*

Peace I leave with you; my peace I give to you.
John 14:27

Whenever the need arises —
at home, at work, or elsewhere —
I will use the following prayer:

As I inhale slowly and deeply, mentally I say,
"I breathe in God's peace"

As I exhale slowly, mentally I say,
"I breathe out tension."

Or

As I inhale slowly and deeply, mentally I say,
"I breathe in God's peace,"

As I exhale slowly, mentally I say,
"I breathe out worry."

After doing this for three or five minutes,
I will be calm, clear, and centered
with God's peace.

As I calm my inner self and breathe in God's peace,
God will envelop me
with the embrace of His peace.

B. The Commotion Within

a. Why all the commotion

Amen, amen, I say to you, you will weep and mourn, while the world rejoices; you will grieve, but your grief will become joy. John 16:20

As inner reactions to a person, event, or situation, my emotions are gauges that inform or warn me about what is happening.

My emotions also provide me with opportunities for building internal strength and for prayer.

My emotions have a life of their own, an intelligence of their own.

The emotional flow of my life is like:

- the engine in my car
- the wind in my sail
- the colors in my favorite painting
- the rhythm in my favorite music
- the love I have for others.

I will respect and accept the flow of my emotions.

b. *Praying with the commotion*

Rejoice in hope,
endure in affliction,
persevere in prayer. Rom 12:12

Because my emotions are non-rational, non-logical,
there's no need to understand or describe them clearly.

Because I have no direct control over my emotions,
I will deal with them indirectly

Because my emotional states are temporary,
I will allow time for them to quiet down, cool down.

Because all my emotions are God-given and good,
I will accept all my emotions, even negative ones.

I will remind myself that there is no need
for guilt feelings
for having negative emotions,
because all my emotions are good.

I will pray with my emotions,
from my emotions,
and because of my emotions.

Because the best prayers come from the heart,
I will speak to God from my heart.

c. Can emotions block my prayer?

Neither death, nor life, nor angels, nor principalities, nor present things, nor future things, nor powers, nor height, nor depth, nor any other creature will be able to separate us from the love of God in Christ Jesus our Lord. Rom 8:38-39

None of my emotions can stop me from praying.

Like physical pain, my negative emotions are unpleasant and undesirable, but absolutely necessary for my survival, growth, and development.

Fear triggers my flight or fight response, which helps me to survive physically, psychologically, and spiritually.

Fear of consequences motivates me to get something done, and enables me to do it quickly to meet a deadline.

Hurt feelings and disappointments can help me to strengthen my relationships.

Feelings of depression can help me to develop internal and spiritual strength.

I will respect and accept all my negative emotions as helpful gauges for surviving, growing, and improving my skills, and helping my prayer life.

d. Dealing with my emotions

Let all bitterness and wrath
and anger and clamor and slander
be put away from you, with all malice. Eph 4:31

I will use healthy outlets for my strong emotions:

- exercise or sports
- craft or hobby
- the arts
- talking it out with a friend
- positive humor.

Because I have no direct control over my emotions,
I will deal with them indirectly.

Dealing with my emotions directly makes
them stronger or last longer.

The best way of removing the air from a container
is to fill the container with water.

I will remove my negative feelings by replacing them
with other feelings by doing something
that holds my total attention, or by praying.

I will change the way I feel by changing what I'm
thinking, saying, or doing, or by praying.

e. *Directing the inner flow for prayer*

Persevere in prayer,
being watchful in it
with thanksgiving. Col 4:2

I can direct the flow of my emotions by:
- focusing my attention on this or that,
- talking about this or that,
- doing this or that.

I will gain greater control over my emotions by directing the use of my:

external senses
— sight, hearing, touch, taste, smell

inner faculties
— simple reasoning, memory, imagination, emotions

spiritual powers
— intellect and free will.

I will learn to direct the flow of my emotions to preserve my peace within and to pray better.

I will use the relaxation technique of slow deep breathing to calm the commotion within for praying better.

*I was regretting the past and
fearing the future.*

*Suddenly God was speaking:
"My Name is I AM."*

*I waited. God continued:
"When you live in the past, with
its mistakes and regrets, it is hard;
I am not there.
My Name is not I Was".*

*"When you live in the future, with
its problems and fears, it is hard;
I am not there.
My Name is not I Will Be".*

*"When you live in this moment,
it is not hard; I am here.
My Name is "I AM. "*

Helen Mallicoat

C. Obstacles to Prayer

a. The God of reality

God said to Moses, "I AM WHO I AM"
Ex. 3:14

The past events of my life no longer exist:
- They're gone.
- The future does not actually exist.
- It may exist in my mind or imagination
  only as thoughts or imaginings.

Because God is present within me this moment,
I pray to God here and now.

b. Self-made obstacles

My grace is sufficient for you, for my power is made perfect in weakness. 2 Cor 12:9

Focusing on:
- my mistakes
- my weaknesses
- mistreatment from others
- injustices suffered
- will lead me to self-pity.

Seeking pity by telling others
about my struggles and misfortunes
leads me to self-pity.

Because God cannot be found in the mud of self-pity,
I will focus on God present within me.

Because of God's immense love for me,
I will pray to God present within me.

c. A forgiving God

For you, 0 Lord, are good and forgiving,
abounding in kindness
to all who call upon you. Psalm 86:5

After seeking forgiveness from God for my sins,
I will let go of my guilt feelings.

If God forgives me,
why should I refuse to forgive myself -
that is, refuse to let go of my guilt feelings?

I will not allow feelings of guilt
to deter me from praying,
because I refuse to focus on my sins.

When feelings of guilt return,
I will thank God for His forgiveness,
and talk to Him about other things.

Because God is so loving and merciful,
I will never allow my sins or guilt
to prevent me from praying.

d. Dealing with distractions

Rejoice always.
Pray without ceasing.
In all circumstances give thanks. 1 Thes 5:16-18

Distractions during prayer
frustrate and discourage many people.

Because prayer is mainly a union of my will
with God's will, I am still praying
if my distractions are not deliberate.

Because God knows I do not have complete control
over my mind and thoughts,
He accepts my distractions
as part of my prayer.

Because distractions are part of my praying,
I will never allow distractions
to discourage me from praying.

I will do slow deep breathing to calm my inner
self as a preparation for praying.

While praying,
if I do my best,
God will do the rest.

e. God here and now

Behold, now is the acceptable time;
behold, now is the day of salvation. 2 Cor 6:2

Because past events and future events
do not exist in reality,
I will find the God of reality
only in the present.

Living in the present moment
keeps me in touch
with God here and now.

God invented the flow of time
to prevent everything from happening
all at once.

Because the present moment is small and manageable,
praying here and now is easy and manageable.

Because God is "I AM",
in the present moment,
I pray to God here and now.

Though distress and anguish have come upon me, your commands are my delight.

Psalm 119:143

$\mathcal{D}$. Radiance Through Prayer

a. Understanding prayer - (t/f Quiz 5)

1 ◯ Distractions during prayer are natural and normal.

2 ◯ Our daily living should be brought into our praying.

3 ◯ Praying is easy to do.

4 ◯ Inner restlessness indicates a need for prayer.

5 ◯ The way we live affects the way we pray.

6 ◯ Prayer is mainly a union of minds with God.

Answers

1. **True**. Distractions during prayer are natural and normal. **True.** We do not have complete control over our mind, and God knows this.

2. **True**. Our daily living should be brought into our praying. **True**. The needs and incidents of daily living provide the contents of our prayers.

3. **True**. Praying is easy to do. **True**. Praying is just as easy as playing golf badly or playing tennis badly. But praying well is difficult, just as playing golf well or playing tennis well is difficult.

4. **True**. Inner restlessness indicates a need for prayer. **True**. Inner restlessness results from a guilty conscience or stress or worry.

5. **True**. The way we live affects the way we pray. **True**. A sinful life makes praying difficult. A hectic, chaotic life make praying difficult. In these situations, prayer is needed to seek forgiveness, for inner peace, or for God's help.

6. **False**. Prayer is mainly a spiritual union of minds with God. **False**. Prayer is mainly a union of *wills* with God, and secondarily a union of minds with God. The essence of prayer is *intention* (from the will), not attention. This the reason that distractions do not end our prayer. We stop praying only when we deliberately decide to stop praying. God knows we do not have complete control over our mind. Do not expect more of yourself than what God expects of you.

7 ◯ The goal of prayer is to possess God.

8 ◯ Praying is both simple and complex.

9 ◯ Progress in prayer means becoming more active during prayer.

10 ◯ Giving reasons is important in prayer.

11 ◯ God answers every prayer in a positive way.

12 ◯ God speaks back to us during prayer.

Answers

7. False. The goal of prayer is to possess God. **False**. How can a drop of water contain the ocean? The goal of prayer is to be possessed by God.

8. True. Praying is both simple and complex. **True**. Praying itself is simple, but we are complex beings. Praying can be simple, but with complicated factors involved such as: the degree of faith, humility, love; the motive or intentions; the preparation.

9. False. Progress in prayer means becoming more active during prayer. **False**. Progress in prayer means becoming more simple and passive during prayer. The highest form of prayer is achieved when a person is completely passive to allow the Holy Spirit to pray in and through that person. God draws a person from active contemplation into passive contemplation.

10. True. Giving reasons is important in prayer. **True**. When asking God for others and for self, we should reason with God even though He already knows the reasons. Doing this will prolong prayer and deepen prayer.

11. True. God answers every prayer in a positive way.
True. ("No" from God is a negative response.)
God answers every prayer in a positive way by:
    a. giving us what we ask for; or
    b. giving it to us later; or
    c. giving us something else instead.

12. True. God speaks back to us during prayer. **True**. God responds to us by influencing our mind, emotions, memory, imagination, or will.

b. *Some notes on prayer*

Getting started

If you're one of those who feel as though you don't pray well, I think the following, based on the writing of Abbot John Chapman (1862-1932), might be of some help.

1. Pray as you can, and don't try to pray as you cannot Take yourself as you find yourself.

2. The only way to pray is to pray; and the way to pray well is to pray much. The less one prays the worse it goes.

If you have no time to pray much at least pray regularly.

3. If you must put up with the fact that when you do try to pray, you can't seem to get into it, then let your prayer consist of telling this to God.

4. Begin wherever you find yourself. Make any acts you want to make and feel you ought to make, but do not force yourself into, feelings of any kind.

5. If you don't know what to do when you have a quarter of an hour alone in Church, then shut out everything else and just give yourself to God and beg Him to have mercy on you and offer Him all your distractions.

6. You can't get rid of the worries of this world or of the questionings of the intellect, but you can laugh at them. Laugh at yourself and then think of God. In the simple relation you have with God by prayer, it is as though you are in the center of a wheel where the noise of the revolving circumference does not matter.

Having the right intention

1. Pray in order to give yourself to God.

2. Pure prayer is a prayer of the will; it is pure intention without words. Do not worry about what you should think or feel. Think about your intention to give yourself to God, cling to Him. Feelings are useful for beginners, but they are not to be depended on. Do not mind if you don't feel love of God or whether you feel commotion or rebellion. Just pray that you may cling to God in absolute detachment. Reason is necessary for theology and ordinary conduct but in prayer it is only useful for beginners. You do not have to reason that God is to be loved, except in the early stages.

3. Want what He wants. Inner quiet is necessary for peace. But if God does not wish us to have peace we must be satisfied with confusion. So do not worry about reasoning your way into God's presence, which is peace of an elusive kind.

4. If we prayed simply because we wanted the "consolations of religion," the state of things would be very disappointing. But if we pray in order to give ourselves to God just as we are, then our imperfections at prayer at any given moment are what God wants. Granted it is not the very best we can do, but in general it is the only kind of prayer we can pray. Even if it is far from what we want, it is what God wants.

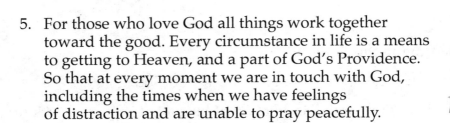

5. For those who love God all things work together toward the good. Every circumstance in life is a means to getting to Heaven, and a part of God's Providence. So that at every moment we are in touch with God, including the times when we have feelings of distraction and are unable to pray peacefully.

6. Minimize what happens in your own soul and maximize God's love for you. Do not think that distraction, dryness and desolation are merely stages of a trial which you pass through on your way to perfection. Perfection in this world is not a calm union with God, unless God so wishes. Jesus suffered temptation and desolation to show us that they are not incompatible with perfection, but in fact are part of perfection. Progress will be made when we become more and more indifferent as to what state we are in.

Do not try to be simple, God does that for you.

Your part is:
*   - to think of others;*
*   - to be with God;*
*   - to avoid thinking about your own*
*   "spiritual state."*

7. Simply be what God enables you to be at this moment. God is not only in every external event, but in every internal event, in every involuntary feeling you have — at every moment in your life you are in touch with God, and His hand is on you. You have only to be carried in His arms. Your one care must be not to jump free and try to walk alone; and finally when you are certain of His love, enjoy the Lord.

You need not expect to be successful in these efforts. You need only to repeat that you want God's will.

And if you must bear some form of suffering, physical, emotional or mental, do not get down on yourself. It is not against perfection to feel that suffering is intolerable, and it is all right to tell God that it is intolerable. Only try with the highest part of you to trust Him and be willing to suffer as long as He chooses, knowing that He will give you the necessary grace.

c. The healing power of God within me

Do you not know that you are the temple of God, and that the Spirit of God dwells in you? I Cor 3:16

Because God is within me
at the center of my soul,
I will allow Him to heal me from within.

For I, the Lord, am your healer. Ex. 15:26

Because God is within me,
at the center of my soul,
I will seek Him within myself through prayer.

Because God is found in the midst of peace,
I will calm my inner self
with slow deep breathing
before praying.

Because God within awaits and welcomes me,
I will seek Him within myself through prayer,
often, anywhere, and anytime.

Because God within loves everyone,
I will let His love flow out
from me to everyone.

d. *The treasure within*

Let nothing disturb you;
nothing cause you fear; all things pass.

God is unchanging. Patience obtains all;
who ever has God needs nothing else.
God alone suffices.

Through prayer, my union with God within me will:
- heal the wounds of my past pains
- purify me of arrogance and selfishness
- increase my inner strength and courage
- teach me patience and endurance
- deepen my faith and trust in God
- give me peace of mind, peace of heart, and peace of soul
- expand my love for God and for others.

Through daily prayer, I will go to God within me:
- to seek help for others and for self
- to seek refuge in times of trouble
- to receive God's gifts and blessings
- to enjoy the spiritual peace He gives
- to share in God's life, light, and love.

How great is your goodness, O Lord,
which you have in store for those who fear you.
Psalm 31:20

e. Being open to God

Because prayer opens my mind, heart, and soul to God,
I will receive God's Goodness through prayer.
I can use any one of these, or make up my own.

God's Peace

As I inhale slowly and deeply, mentally I say,

I breathe in God's peace,

As I exhale slowly, mentally I say,

I breathe out tension.

As I inhale slowly and deeply, mentally I say,

I breathe in God's peace,

As I exhale slowly, mentally I say,

I breathe out worry.

As I inhale slowly and deeply, mentally I say,

I breathe in God's peace,

As I exhale slowly, mentally I say,

I breathe out anxiety.

As I inhale slowly and deeply, mentally I say,

I breathe in God's peace,

As I exhale slowly, mentally I say,

I breathe out my fears.

As I inhale slowly and deeply, mentally I say,
I breathe in God's peace,

As I exhale slowly, mentally I say,
I breathe out irritation.

As I inhale slowly and deeply, mentally I say,
I breathe in God's peace,

As I exhale slowly, mentally I say,
I breathe out turmoil.

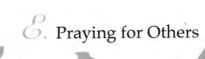

8. Praying for Others

a. *Toxic grudges*

> *But if you do not forgive men their trespasses,*
> *neither will your Father forgive your trespasses.*
> *Mt 6:15*

Holding a grudge against someone is
like trying to harm him by taking poison a little at a time —
it harms me instead,
without harming him.

The more I focus on a grudge,
the more its poison seeps into my soul,
and blocks my prayer.

Because grudges destroy my inner peace,
I will let go of them to preserve my peace within,
and to pray from my heart.

Letting go of grudges by focusing my attention on
the positive aspects of my life
also set others at peace.

I will open my heart to forgive,
so my heart will be open
to receive God's forgiveness.

b. Praying for my foes

You have heard it said, "You shall love your
neighbor and hate your enemy". But I say to
you, love your enemies, pray for those who
persecute you, that you may be children
of your heavenly Father. Mt 5: 44-45

Because all emotions are good,
I will learn to accept
the negative emotions of others
without becoming defensive.

I will learn to deflect criticisms or harsh words
directed at me by not taking them in a personal way.

I will not descend to the muck of retaliation
when I am offended or hurt by someone.

I will secretly calm myself with slow deep breathing
and breathe in God's peace,
when someone angry or upset confronts me.

I will secretly ask God to calm that person,
and to grant that person peace.

c. The peace of acceptance

Bear one another's burdens,
and so you will fulfill the law of Christ. Gal 6:2

Because the behavior of others is beyond my control,
I will stop trying to change other people.

Because I do not have access to the depths
of a person's emotional life or subconscious,
I will accept and respect people
without trying to understand them better.

Because love cannot be forced but must be freely given,
I will accept the fact that I cannot make a person love me,
or love me more.

Because I cannot make others happy,
I will create a loving atmosphere
wherein others can be happy
if they choose to be happy.

Because God accepts me as I am,
I will accept others as they are.

d. Prayers of love

And this is my prayer:
that your love may increase ever more
and more in knowledge and every kind of
perception,to discern what is of value, so
that you may be pure and blameless for the day
of Christ,filled with the fruit of righteousness
that comes through Jesus Christ
for glory and praise of God. Phil 1:9

The more I love others:
- the more I worry about them
- the more I suffer with them when they suffer
- the more I sacrifice for them
- the more vulnerable I become
- the more sensitive I become
- the more I pray for them.

Because God loves with an infinite love the ones I love,
I will place them in God's loving care daily.

I will accept the negative emotions of anger, frustration,
and disappointment that come with loving.

I will accept the negative thoughts and judgments
that come with loving.

Through prayer, God's love will cushion the lower lows
that love brings me, and elevate the higher highs that
come with loving.

e. *Bonding better through prayer*

Let love be sincere;
hate what is evil, hold on to what is good;
love one another with mutual affection;
anticipate one another in showing honor.
Rom 12:9

Because I cannot change another person,
to improve our relationship
I will focus on changing myself.

To improve any of my relationships,

I have to change myself:
- my expectations
- my reactions and responses
- my attitudes
- my words and actions
- through daily prayer.

Because nagging begets resentment and resistance,
I will limit the number of my kindly reminders.

Accepting others without pressuring them to change
sets me at peace,
and sets them at peace.

By receiving God's peace through daily prayer,
I will become a channel of peace to others.

Preserving my peace within through prayer
will make me easier to work with,
and easier to live with.

f. The way of forgiveness

For if you forgive men their trespasses,
your heavenly Father also will forgive you.
Mt 6:14

If I refuse to forgive someone,
the toxic resentment and grudge
will poison my inner peace.

Forgiveness does not come from my feelings.
Forgiveness does not come from my mind.
Forgiveness comes from my will.

Once I have freely chosen to forgive someone
by a decision of my will,
the negative feelings and critical thoughts I have
do not matter.

I will allow these natural negative feelings and
critical thoughts to come and go.

Forgiving a person will open up my mind, heart,
and spirit for receiving love from God and from others.

The way of forgiveness leads me to God
Who is within me.

Be kind to one another, compassionate,
forgiving one another as God has forgiven you.
Eph 4:32

g. The art of loving

For God did not give us a spirit of cowardice,
but rather of power and love and self-control.
2 Tim 1:7

Because loving involves the giving of myself,
I will gain greater control over myself
to improve my ability to love.

Because loving goes beyond my thoughts and feelings,
I will rise to the level of will and behavior.

Because loving includes critical thoughts and negative feelings,
I will rise above them to the level
of supportive words and acts of kindness.

Because loving is a commitment — a big complex decision
that includes a set of positive decisions, positive attitudes,
and positive behavior over a long period of time —
I will accept the hurts, the bad, and the ugly
along with the joy, delight, and fulfillment of loving.

In and through prayer,
God will teach me how to love as He loves.

I give you a new commandment:
love one another;
just as I have loved you,
you also must love one another.
John 13:34

I am the Light of the world.

John 8:12

ℱ. The Radiance of God Within

a. God's peace

> *May the Lord of peace himself*
> *give you peace at all times and in every way.*
> *2 Thes 3:16*

Whenever the need arises -- at home, at work, or elsewhere
I will use the following prayer:

As I inhale slowly and deeply, mentally I say,
   I breathe in God's peace,

As I exhale slowly, mentally I say,
   I breathe out tension.

Or

As I inhale slowly and deeply, mentally I say,
   I breathe in God's peace,

As I exhale slowly, mentally I say,
   I breathe out worry.

After doing this for three or five minutes,
I will be calm, clear, and centered with God's peace.

As I calm my inner self
and breathe in God's peace,
God will envelop me
with the embrace of His peace.

b. God's light

For you were once darkness, but now you are light in the Lord. Live as children of light, for light produces every kind of goodness and righteousness and truth. Eph 5:8-9

Whenever the need arises -- at home, at work, or elsewhere I will use the following prayer:

As I inhale slowly and deeply, mentally I say,

I breathe in God's light,

As I exhale slowly, mentally I say,

I breathe out darkness.

Or

As I inhale slowly and deeply, mentally I say,

I breathe in God's light,

As I exhale slowly, mentally I say,

I breathe out my gloom.

After doing this for three or five minutes, I will be calm, clear, and centered with God's peace.

As I calm my inner self
and breathe in God's light,
God will envelop me
with the radiance of His light.

c. God's wisdom

All wisdom comes from God
and is with him forever. Sirach 1:1

Whenever the need arises -- at home, at work,
or elsewhere I will use the following prayer:

As I inhale slowly and deeply, mentally I say,
I breathe in God's wisdom,

As I exhale slowly, mentally I say,
I breathe out confusion.

Or

As I inhale slowly and deeply, mentally I say,
I breathe in God's wisdom,

As I exhale slowly, mentally I say,
I breathe out ignorance.

After doing this for three or five minutes,
I will be calm, clear, and centered with God's peace.

As I calm my inner self
and breathe in God's wisdom,
I will be more open to
God's wisdom and guidance.

For wisdom is better than jewels, and all that you may desire cannot compare with her.

Prov 8:11

d. God's strength

The Almighty — we cannot find him;
he is great in power and justice,
righteousness he will not violate. Job 37:23

Whenever the need arises -- at home, at work,
or elsewhere I will use the following prayer:

As I inhale slowly and deeply, mentally I say,
I breathe in God's strength,

As I exhale slowly, mentally I say,
I breathe out weakness.

Or

As I inhale slowly and deeply, mentally I say,
I breathe in God's strength,

As I exhale slowly, mentally I say,
I breathe out fatigue.

After doing this for three or five minutes,
I will be stronger with God's strength.

As I calm my inner self
and breathe in God's strength,
I will be more open to God's strength
in my heart and soul.

e. God's love

I have loved you with an everlasting love;
Therefore, I have continued my faithfulness
to you. Jer 31:3

Because God is within me,
at the center of my soul,
with His immense love for me,
I am surrounded by His love.

As I inhale slowly and deeply, mentally I say,

I breathe in God's love,

As I exhale slowly, mentally I say,

I breathe out anger.

Or

As I inhale slowly and deeply, mentally I say,

I breathe in God's love,

As I exhale slowly, mentally I say,

I breathe out frustration.

As I calm my inner self
and breathe in God's love,
God will embrace me
with the warmth of His love.

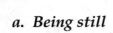
G. Radiance with God's Brightness

a. *Being still*

Be still, and know that I am God. Psalm 46:10

Through prayer,
I will transform daily stress into a power-source
for my commitment to my loved ones,
and the challenge of my own growth
and development.

With my regular nightly practice
of relaxing my body
and calming my inner self
before getting into bed,
I will be still enough to experience my inner peace,
and fall asleep in God's arms.

With my daily use of the slow deep breathing technique,
I will be calm, clear, and centered with God's peace.

I will use relaxation techniques daily
to calm my mind, emotions, and heart,
to find and experience God within me.

Because the only obstacle to finding God
in and through prayer is myself,
by not praying. Therefore, I will pray daily and often.

b. APT living for God

I will be like the wise sailor of a sail boat in choppy seas,
who makes full use of all that is within his control,
with total trust in God,
instead of focusing on the forces of the wind and waves
that are beyond his control.

Because everything I do affects and forms
my thoughts, feelings, and character,
I will focus on fulfilling my daily tasks well
and with inner calmness,
for God and for others.

APT living for Loving
— Acceptance of my present situation with
— Purpose in mind for doing well the
— Task at hand - will create the aptitude for:

  - doing quality work,
  - relating well with others,
  - enjoying my life more fully,
  - and being a channel of God's blessings to others.

I will shape and transform myself
into a patient, reliable, loving person
through APT living and through daily prayer.

c. Flowing with God

In him we live and move and have our being.
Acts 17:28

Because daily changes are continuous in my life,
I will flow with these changes like water,
and work with them,
while directing my flow toward my spiritual goals.

I will let go of the past and the future
to flow with the present,
so I can deal with what's real and beneficial,
because God is "I AM".
I will flow around the big rocks
(things beyond my control)
by accepting or ignoring them,
while trusting in God's love for me.

I will preserve the peace within the center of my soul,
as I flow with changes up and down, side to side,
while knowing God is always within me.

Because God cares about everything in my life,
I will talk to God about anything and everything.

d. A channel of God's peace

Lord, make me a channel of Your peace.
St. Francis of Assisi

Because of God's love for everyone,
I will accept and show respect to everyone,
to set others at peace.

Because God's forgiveness awaits me,
I will let go of grudges and resentment,
for internal peace and external peace.

Because God's love is within me,
I will channel my flow of patience and kindness
to lead others to inner peace.

Because I am a channel of God's peace,
I will reassure and encourage others
with my kind, supportive words,
to allow God's peace to flow out to others.

Because praying will transform me
into a patient, loving person,
I will pray daily and often.

Because our loving God
answers every prayer with a positive response,
I will pray for others and for self
with total trust and confidence.

e. God is love

In him was life,
and the life was the light of men.
The light shines in the darkness,
and the darkness has not overcome it.
John 1:4-5

Because God is
my Life, Light, and Love,
I will draw from His life, light, and love,
present at the center of my soul.

Because God is
Omniscient (all-knowing)
and Omnipotent (all-powerful),
He knows what's best for me and can help me,
I will accept whatever He allows to happen to me.

Because God is
verified by His goodness and beauty
in His creation, I will strive to link all goodness
and beauty with God's goodness and beauty.

Because God is
everywhere, in myself and in others,
I will show respect to God
in others and in myself.

f. God within me

Do you not know that you are the temple of God, and that the Spirit of God dwells in you? I Cor 3:16

Because God is within me,
at the center of my soul,
I will seek Him within myself through prayer.

Because God is found in the midst of peace,
I will calm my inner self
with slow deep breathing
before praying.

Because God within awaits and welcomes me,
I will seek Him within myself through prayer
often, anywhere, and anytime.

Because God within loves everyone,
I will let His love flow out from me to everyone.

g. The Guest within

In the same way the Spirit too comes to the aid of our weakness; for we do not know how to pray as we ought, but the Spirit itself intercedes with inexpressible groanings. Rom 8:26

Come, Holy Spirit,

>Replace the tension within us
>with a holy relaxation.

>Replace the turbulence within us
>with a sacred calm.

>Replace the anxiety within us
>with a quiet confidence.

>Replace the fear within us
>with a strong faith.

>Replace the bitterness within us
>with the sweetness of grace.

>Replace the darkness within us
>with a gentle light.

>Replace the coldness within us
>with a loving warmth.

>Replace the night within us
>with Your day.

Replace the winter within us
with Your spring.

Straighten our crookedness,
fill our emptiness.

Dull the edge of our pride,
smooth the flow of our humbleness.

Illumine the light of our love,
quench the - flames of our lust.

Let us see ourselves as You see us,
that we may see You as You have promised,
and be fortunate according to Your word:

Blessed are the pure of heart,
for they shall see God. Mt 5:8
Amen

h. Receiving God's goodness

Let nothing disturb you;
nothing cause you fear; all things pass.
God is unchanging. Patience obtains all;
whoever has God needs nothing else.
God alone suffices.
(Bookmark of St.Teresa of Avila)

Through prayer, my union with God within me will:
- heal the wounds of my past pains
- purify me of arrogance and selfishness
- increase my inner strength and courage
- teach me patience and endurance
- deepen my faith and trust in God
- give me peace of mind, peace of heart, and peace of soul
- expand my love for God and for others.

Through daily prayer, I will go to God within me:
- to seek help for others and for self
- to seek refuge in times of trouble
- to receive God's gifts and blessings
- to enjoy the spiritual peace He gives
- to share in God's life, light, and love.

How great is your goodness, O Lord,
which you have in store
for those who fear you. Psalm 31:20

May the God of hope fill you with all joy and peace in believing, so that you may abound in hope by the power of the Holy Spirit.

Rom 15:13

a. God's light

As I inhale slowly and deeply, mentally I say,
I breathe in God's light,

As I exhale slowly, mentally I say,
I breathe out darkness.

As I inhale slowly and deeply, mentally I say,
I breathe in God's light,

As I exhale slowly, mentally I say,
I breathe out sadness.

As I inhale slowly and deeply, mentally I say,
I breathe in God's light,

As I exhale slowly, mentally I say,
I breathe out my gloom.

As I inhale slowly and deeply, mentally I say,
I breathe in God's light,

As I exhale slowly, mentally I say,
I breathe out blindness.

b. God's wisdom

As I inhale slowly and deeply, mentally I say,
I breathe in God's wisdom,

As I exhale slowly, mentally I say,
I breathe out confusion.

As I inhale slowly and deeply, mentally I say,
I breathe in God's wisdom,

As I exhale slowly, mentally I say,
I breathe out ignorance.

As I inhale slowly and deeply, mentally I say,
I breathe in God's wisdom,

As I exhale slowly, mentally I say,
I breathe out hurtful words.

As I inhale slowly and deeply, mentally I say,
I breathe in God's wisdom,

As I exhale slowly, mentally I say,
I breathe out stupidity.

c. God's strength

As I inhale slowly and deeply, mentally I say,
I breathe in God's strength,

As I exhale slowly, mentally I say,
I breathe out weakness.

As I inhale slowly and deeply, mentally I say,
I breathe in God's strength,

As I exhale slowly, mentally I say,
I breathe out fatigue.

As I inhale slowly and deeply, mentally I say,
I breathe in God's power,

As I exhale slowly, mentally I say,
I breathe out helplessness.

As I inhale slowly and deeply, mentally I say,
I breathe in God's power,

As I exhale slowly, mentally I say,
I breathe out cowardice.

d. God's love

As I breathe in slowly and deeply, mentally I say,
I breathe in God's love,

As I breathe out slowly and deeply, mentally I say,
I breathe out anger.

As I inhale slowly and deeply, mentally I say,
I breathe in God's love,

As I exhale slowly, mentally I say,
I breathe out frustration.

As I inhale slowly and deeply, mentally I say,
I breathe in God's love,

As I exhale slowly, mentally I say,
I breathe out loneliness.

As I inhale slowly and deeply, mentally I say,
I breathe in God's love,

As I exhale slowly, mentally I say,
I breathe out restlessness.

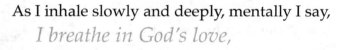

As I inhale slowly and deeply, mentally I say,
I breathe in God's love,

As I exhale slowly, mentally I say,
I breathe out emptiness.

As I inhale slowly and deeply, mentally I say,
I breathe in God's love,

As I exhale slowly, mentally I say,
I breathe out selfishness.

As I inhale slowly and deeply, mentally I say,
I breathe in God's love,

As I exhale slowly, mentally I say,
I breathe out anguish.

e. God's truth and justice

As I inhale slowly and deeply, mentally I say,
I breathe in Gods truth,

As I exhale slowly, mentally I say,
I breathe out deceit.

As I inhale slowly and deeply, mentally I say,
I breathe in God's truth,

As I exhale slowly, mentally I say,
I breathe out lying.

As I inhale slowly and deeply, mentally I say,
I breathe in God's justice,

As I exhale slowly, mentally I say,
I breathe out injustice.

As I inhale slowly and deeply, mentally I say,
I breathe in God's justice,

As I exhale slowly, mentally I say,
I breathe out unfairness.

As I inhale slowly and deeply, mentally I say,
I breathe in God's humbleness,

As I exhale slowly, mentally I say,
I breathe out arrogance and pride.

f. God's joy and purity

As I inhale slowly and deeply, mentally I say,
I breathe in God's joy,

As I exhale slowly, mentally I say,
I breathe out sadness.

As I inhale slowly and deeply, mentally I say,
I breathe in God's joy and peace,

As I exhale slowly, mentally I say,
I breathe out disappointment.

As I inhale slowly and deeply, mentally I say,
I breathe in God's purity,

As I exhale slowly, mentally I say,
I breathe out impurity.

As I inhale slowly and deeply, mentally I say,
I breathe in God's purity,

As I exhale slowly, mentally I say,
I breathe out negativity.

g. God's beauty

As I breathe in slowly and deeply, mentally I say,
   I breathe in God's beauty,

As I breathe out slowly and deeply, mentally I say,
   I breathe out disorder.

As I inhale slowly and deeply, mentally I say,
   I breathe in God's beauty,

As I exhale slowly, mentally I say,
   I breathe out ugliness.

As I inhale slowly and deeply, mentally I say,
   I breathe in God's creativeness,

As I exhale slowly, mentally I say,
   I breathe out my dullness.

As I inhale slowly and deeply, mentally I say,
   I breathe in God's creativeness,

As I exhale slowly, mentally I say,
   I breathe out my blandness.

Lord, make me a channel of Your peace.

St. Francis of Assisi

Index

Bible Quotes

Acts	17:28	*In him we live and move and have our being.* (194)
Colossians Col	4:2	*Persevere in prayer, being watchful in it with thanksgiving.* (158)
1 Corinthians 1 Cor	3:16	*Do you not know that you are the temple of God, and that the Spirit of God dwells in you?* (174, 197)
	6:19	*Do you not know that your body is a temple of the Holy Spirit within you, whom you have from God, and that you are not your own?* (150)
	6:20	*Therefore, glorify God in your body.* (150)
2 Corinthians 2 Cor	6:2	*Behold, now is the acceptable time; behold, now is the day of salvation.* (164)
	12:9	*My grace is sufficient for you, for my power is made perfect in weakness.* (161)
Ephesians Eph	4:31	*Let all bitterness and wrath and anger and clamor and slander be put away from you, with all malice.* (157)
	4:32	*Be kind to one another, compassionate, forgiving one another as God has forgiven you.* (183)
	5: 8-9	*For you were once darkness, but now you are light in the Lord. Live as children of light, for light produces every kind of goodness and righteousness and truth.* (187)

Mark	4:39	*"Quiet! Be still!" The wind ceased and there was a great calm.* **(152)**
	13:13	*Take heed, watch and pray.* **(146)**
Mathew Mt	5:8	*Blessed are the pure of heart, for they shall see God.* **(199)**
	5: 44-45	*You have heard it said, "You shall love your neighbor and hate your enemy." But I say to you, love your enemies, pray for those who persecute you, that you may be children of your heavenly Father.* **(179)**
	6:14	*For if you forgive men their trespasses, your heavenly Father also will forgive you.* **(127, 183)**
	6:15	*But if you do not forgive men their trespasses, neither will your Father forgive your trespasses.* **(178)**
Micah	6:8	*He has showed you, O man, what is good; and what does the Lord require of you but to do justice, and to love kindness, and to walk humbly with your God.* **(193)**

Philippians Phil	1:9	*And this is my prayer: that your love may increase ever more and more in knowledge and every kind of perception, to discern what is of value, so that you may be pure and blameless for the day of Christ, filled with the fruit of righteousness that comes through Jesus Christ for glory and praise of God.* (181)
Proverbs Pro	8:11	*For wisdom is better than jewels, and all that you may desire cannot compare with her.* (189)
Psalms	27:1	*The Lord is my light and my salvation; whom should I fear? The Lord is my life's refuge; of whom should I be afraid?* (147)
	31:20	*How great is your goodness, O Lord, which you have in store for those who fear you.* (175, 200)
	46:10	*Be still, and know that I am God.* (192)
	85:5	*For you, O Lord, are good and forgiving, abounding in kindness to all who call upon you.* (162)
	119:143	*Though distress and anguish have come upon me, your commands are my delight.* (165)

Romans	8:26	*In the same way the Spirit too comes to the aid of our weakness; for we do not know how to pray as we ought, but the Spirit itself intercedes with inexpressible groanings.* **(198)**
	8: 38-39	*Neither death, nor life, nor angels, no principalities, now present things, nor depth, nor any other creature will be able to separate us from the love of God in Christ Jesus our Lord.* **(156)**
	12:9	*Let love be sincere; hate what is evil, hold ono what is good; love one another with mutual affection, anticipate one another in showing honor.* **(182)**
	12:12	*Rejoice in hope, endure in affliction, persevere in prayer.* **(155)**
	15:13	*May the God of hope fill you with all joy and peace in believing, so that you may abound in hope by the power of the Holy Spirit.* **(201)**
Sirach	1:1	*All wisdom comes from God and is with him forever.* **(188)**
1 Thessalonians 1 Thes	5: 16-18	*Rejoice always. Pray without ceasing. In all circumstances give thanks.* **(163)**
2 Thessalonians 2 Thes	3:16	*May the Lord of peace himself give you peace at all times and in every way.* **(186)**
2 Timothy 2 Tim	1:7	*For God did not give us a spirit of cowardice, but rather of power and love and self-control.* **(184)**

The Small Steps to Radiance

"Heal" comes from the Greek, root "kailo" and the angle-saxon root "hal", which are also the roots for "healthy", whole" and "holy". These are the small steps to being healed, healthy, whole, holy.

～ Daily reminders ～

1. All my negative emotions are good, beneficial.
2. All my stress is good, beneficial.
3. I can improve all my relationships, even the worst one.
4. I will allow God within me to heal me from within.

～ Daily behavior ～

1. I will accept all negative emotions in myself and in others.
2. I will use stress as motivating energy for helping others and self.
3. I will do centering prayer at least twice a day to let
   God heal me from within.

～ Daily therapy ～

A. I will use the relaxation technique nightly before bed:

   1. to dissolve the residual effects of daily stress;
   2. to get a better night's rest for a fresh start the next morning;
   3. to allow my brain, nervous system, emotions,
      and body to repair themselves during sleep;
   4. to let God heal me from within during sleep.

B. I will use APT living:

   Acceptance of every situation for the
   Purpose of helping others and self by doing well the
   Task at hand here and now.

CPSIA information can be obtained
at www.ICGtesting.com
Printed in the USA
FSHW04n1245220418
47081FS

9 780692 979020